LAURA ASHLEY

Decorating
CHILDREN'S ROOMS

LAURA ASHLEY
Decorating
CHILDREN'S ROOMS

CREATING FUN, PRACTICAL AND SAFE
SURROUNDINGS FOR YOUR CHILD

JOANNA COPESTICK
Special photography by Lucinda Symons

CROWN TRADE PAPERBACKS
NEW YORK

Step-by-step text by Alison Wormleighton

Edited by Alison Wormleighton
Designed by Christine Wood
Special photography by Lucinda Symons
Styling by Lucy Elworthy
Illustrations by Kate Simuneck

First published in the United Kingdom in 1996 by Ebury Press
Random House, 20 Vauxhall Bridge Road, London SW1V 2SA

Published by Crown Trade Paperbacks, 201 East 50th Street,
New York, New York 10022. Member of the Crown Publishing Group.

Random House, Inc. New York, Toronto, London, Sydney, Auckland

http://www.randomhouse.com/

CROWN TRADE PAPERBACKS and colophon are trademarks of
Crown Publishers, Inc.

Manufactured in Great Britain by Butler and Tanner Lt, Frome, Somerset

Library of Congress Cataloging-in-Publication Data is available on request

ISBN 0-517-88732-0

10 9 8 7 6 5 4 3 2 1

First American Edition

Contents

Introduction

The family and home were central to Laura Ashley's life. With four children, she had to give the decoration of nurseries and children's rooms a lot of thought, and the Victorian nursery was Laura Ashley's main source of inspiration. She wanted to re-create a traditional nursery that had been part of the house over generations and where successive children had played and enjoyed similar pastimes and hobbies. Many of the original Laura Ashley floral fabrics and wallpapers, such as those used in the little girl's pink bedroom on pages 82–83, were particularly suited to her nostalgic view.

The lifestyles of children today are continually changing and the designs of the Laura Ashley Mother & Child prints reflect this. A child's bedroom must be not only a practical and comfortable environment but also an inspiring place for creative play and learning. Wide pictorial borders or friezes have introduced many different themes to the collection. These themes have been carried through into fabrics and wallpapers to tell a complete story. Also part of the collection are fabrics and wallpapers with simple patterns such as colorful watercolored ginghams, polkadots, and painterly stripes. These coordinate with the rest of the collection, enabling you to create a truly original scheme for your child's bedroom. In this book the themes are traditional but most of the rooms have been decorated in a contemporary style, creating a colorful and jolly environment or a fantasy world.

This book includes a host of ideas for decorating and furnishing different children's rooms. With twenty-five step-by-step projects to help you do the decorating yourself – including some projects that require a child's helping hand – the book will help you not only to prepare for a new baby but also to provide for the needs of a growing child, from toddler to teenager.

Cheerful, busy borders can form the basis for a cohesive decorative scheme. Here, a sapphire blue gingham wallpaper makes a perfect backdrop for shades of mustard and chambray blue. The rag dolls and the building blocks are echoed in motifs in the fabric and in the wallpaper border, designed to look like a children's bookshelf.

CHAPTER ONE

Planning the Basics

Designing a room around the ever-changing whims of children can be quite a challenge, since youngsters cultivate tastes and preferences at a rate that would confound the most ardent and innovative home decorator. But by putting effort into creating a room reminiscent of a traditional and reassuring haven, filled with interest and stimulation in terms of color, pattern, toys, and books, you can encourage successive generations to enjoy the simple pleasures of play.

A child's room is the one place in your house where you can be certain an adventurous decorating scheme will be successful. Walls that incorporate strong color combinations, daring paper borders, and brightly painted furniture and floorboards are just a few of the ways in which you can introduce vibrant color and a lively sense of purpose into a room. You will also be encouraging your child to appreciate the delightful possibilities of color, pattern, and texture, giving him or her a headstart in becoming visually literate – a positive asset in a world where images rather than words dominate.

Fabric is the key in this feminine room. Bold, painterly harlequin checks create a quilt-like feeling for the bedcover and are juxtaposed with white and rose stripes on the bed curtains, while a colorful wallpaper featuring ballet dancers is many a young girl's dream. A box bed such as this is both a cozy retreat and a means of saving space elsewhere in the room.

THE EVOLUTION OF THE NURSERY

The days when children were neither seen nor heard, but spent much of their youth cloistered in a top-floor nursery away from parents, are thankfully long gone. However, the nostalgic image of a Victorian nursery, decorated and equipped with traditional furnishings and toys, still serves as the quintessential blueprint to which many a new parent refers.

The evocative traditional nursery of Victorian times evolved toward the end of the 1800s, when people first began to devote some attention to the decoration and furnishing of children's

Color, inspiration, and a coordinated scheme of nursery rhyme characters prove that the modern-day nursery still incorporates the classic elements of comfort and storage but adds a touch of panache and adventure.

rooms – although the nurseries were not as colorful or inspirational as they are today. A typical Victorian nursery would usually have included a large toy-storage cupboard, a central round table for children to eat their meals at, and some rudimentary cooking facilities. Walls would have been covered with a simply decorated or deep-toned wallpaper, sealed with a glaze as a protective covering against sticky fingers. There may have been a few pictures on the walls. Furniture tended to be reused from elsewhere in the house, often painted white to give it some uniformity.

Equipment specifically designed for the nursery would have included a wooden bassinet (movable crib), cradle and/or crib, a solid rocking horse (in more affluent households), a child-sized washstand, a willow-framed baby carriage, and a cane chair. Gradually, this room became a haven of work, rest, and play where children could spend hours at a time, in a microcosm of an adult's world.

Just as the plain wall decoration of the early nursery slowly succumbed to more ornate wallpaper, so children's toys developed from simple wooden shapes and rag dolls to carefully crafted wooden Noah's arks complete with animals (which were deemed suitable as both toys and lessons in morality), painted building blocks, charming dolls' houses, finely decorated and dressed porcelain dolls, and spinning tops. Books were always introduced to children in the nursery, too.

The same basic components make a successful

nursery today – the only concessions to modern needs being perhaps a dimmer switch and an alarm clock. Otherwise, the timeless appeal of wooden toys, heirloom furniture, and simple furnishings endures.

In addition to the ever-popular traditional elements, modern-day children's rooms also need to perform a variety of functions while providing a stimulating, fun environment in which youngsters can realize their full potential. A child's room needs to fulfill the roles of a sleep place, play area, workroom, and personal space. It must house a variety of toys, a computer, music equipment, clothes, a seating area, and a homework desk.

The main difference between a contemporary young person's room and the Victorian nursery is that today's child does not spend so much time in his or her own room. It is more of a personal place, somewhere to retreat to when they want to play, think, or escape a noisy family. Nowadays, children share the whole of the house with their parents – especially the family room and the kitchen, which, if given a free hand, they may colonize completely with their belongings, and, later on, friends.

PLANNING THE SPACE

The secret of making a child's room one that will be cherished for years to come is to build in a level of flexibility in your decoration, furniture, and curtains. This will allow the room to reflect a child's growth and development with periodic changes. Planning the room with an eye on future needs is particularly useful if you want to avoid having to revamp the scheme too often. Once you have decided on the type and style of furniture, be it old country pine, painted and stenciled new wood, or wood substitutes such as laminate, you can take a few risks when you come to address the decoration of walls and windows, furniture and floor.

Firstly, consider the size and shape of the room and decide how many children it might eventually house – this will affect the type of furniture you should plan to acquire over the next few years. Obviously your decorating decisions will be based on the style of furniture you favor and whether you have one child or more, boys or girls, or both.

Shared bedrooms are often sensible options when space is at a premium or when siblings are quite close in age – youngsters soon learn to appreciate the comfort and security offered by a shared space. As they get older, though, it is important to provide each with an area of the room they can call their own, particularly once they enter the teenage years. Sometimes a decorative screen can be used to section off the room.

Check that there are enough electric outlets in the room – initially for lights, and later on for equipment such as a computer, a television, and a stereo system. You can never have too many electric outlets.

Allocate space for clothes and toy storage. It is more flexible to provide freestanding toy storage, but you could build a closet if there is an alcove in the room.

Decide whether there are any obvious architectural features that you could emphasize and enhance as focal points, such as fireplaces, alcoves, or bay windows.

The space inside an old, disused fireplace can be used for displaying or storing toys or a miniature table and chairs, while window seats placed inside a bay window and fitted with hinged lids provide additional storage space. Children love nooks and crannies in which they can hide, or create miniature worlds with their toys, so make the most of any awkward-shaped corners or built-in cupboards that may already exist in your home.

COLORFUL WALLS AND FLOORS

All children adore bright colors and busy patterns, so seize the chance to be inventive. Create a bright, lively, and fanciful scheme by using large expanses of rich, saturated color on the walls, interspersed with vibrant paper borders, painted wooden paneling, or striped or freehand designs.

You could also try your hand at a simple mural. Decide on an image or scene, possibly based on the theme of the room, such as a nursery rhyme, teddy bears, or ducks, and transfer your image to the wall using graph paper.

Another way of making a dramatic color statement is to divide the wall in half horizontally using two strongly contrasting colors, such as primrose yellow above and a luminous powder blue below. You can either separate the colors with a straight line ranged around the room, or try a more freehand approach and introduce a wavy line, a zigzag formation, or a crenellated edge halfway up the wall. Simply mark out your chosen border with a pencil and steel tape measure, then apply masking tape to all edges before you apply the second color. These are all simple but highly effective ways of introducing panels of strong color into a room.

If your child becomes tired of any one border, you can conceal it by applying a paper border over it to mark the transition between colors, or simply change the color above or below your dividing line. To further emphasize a color scheme, paint freehand borders of color around a favorite picture frame, or punctuate the walls with small display shelves painted in a similar or contrasting color.

For children who are obsessed with drawing, fix a length of hardboard along the bottom edge of one or two walls and paint it with blackboard paint to provide a permanent drawing slate and an ever-changing focal point in the room. Alternatively, apply blackboard paint to the back of freestanding bookshelves as a way of dividing up the space in a room. You could create a reading area using two bookshelves placed at right angles in the corner of the room to form walls and an "entrance." Furnish the corner with miniature wooden chairs, a small round table, and a wicker basket for storing large picture books. Fix peg rails along the walls at chair rail height and suspend fabric or lightweight books from them using colored string or raffia. What better way to encourage nursery readers? Or remove the books and transform the space into a make-believe shop, using the blackboard for drawings of the goods on sale – fruit and vegetables or clothes and toys.

Instead of covering up floorboards with wall-to-wall carpet, treat the floor as a blank canvas on which to paint decorative designs. Older children would love to help paint a checkerboard pattern or chevron border in two or more colors. For babies and toddlers, try painting or stenciling simple motifs such as polkadots, wide and narrow stripes, or farmyard animals. Warm up the room in winter with the addition of a generous-sized rag rug or a traditional painted floorcloth. Or turn the floor into a playground by painting on a hopscotch game or small checkerboard.

Other suitable floor coverings for children's rooms are natural coir, sisal, or seagrass matting, which is hardwearing and durable. It is not so suited to crawling babies, however, as it can be rough on their knees. Cork tiles are a good choice, since they are relatively inexpensive, spill-proof, easy to clean, and warm underfoot; they can be enhanced by the addition of a brightly colored rug or floorcloth.

Try to keep a fair amount of floorspace uncluttered so that children have room to play, as well as a clear area for spreading out the contents of dolls' houses, baskets of small toys, jigsaw puzzles, or a collection of wooden building blocks.

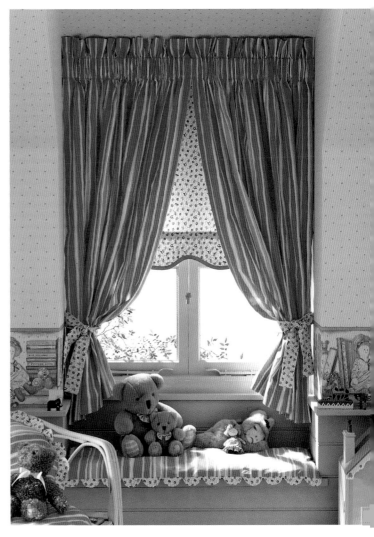

Polkadots, stripes, and nursery motifs combine in a jolly scheme based around the classic nursery colors of sapphire blue and poppy red. Pretty scalloped detailing on the roller shade, window seat cushions, and chair cushion softens edges and draws the look together.

DECORATING WITH FABRIC

Fabric is a key element for providing pattern and color in children's rooms. If you don't want to adorn a baby's nursery in swaths of elaborate chintz – which will quickly pall when your child, aged three years, becomes a whirlwind of energy, desperate to assume the attributes of a miniature adult – select a quite grown-up fabric, such as a checked, striped, or simple floral design, as a starting point. Use an age-related fabric, like a novelty print of ducks, teddy bears, circus clowns, or nursery-rhyme characters, for pillows, duvet covers, roller shades, or draped swags. That way you will only have to replace the smaller items every few years, while the main curtains, upholstery, accent pillows, and bed linen can remain the same for quite a while.

Often it is the small decorative details of a room that linger in children's minds long after they have outgrown their first bedroom. Use fabric for making drawstring bags of varying sizes and hang them on a peg rail to store small toys, bricks, hair bands or ribbons, and general clutter. Or make charming nightdress or pajama bags out of pretty fabric in the shape of animals. Line generous-sized wicker baskets with gingham fabric for versatile toy storage. On open shelves, use fabric to make a tie shade which serves the dual purpose of keeping out the dust and covering up the toys so that they do not lose their novelty value.

Any fabric scraps from family heirlooms such as silk evening gowns or old patchwork quilts can be worked into a bed quilt, wall hanging, or pajama bag. Or make soft toys in simple animal shapes using floral, polkadot, or plain fabric remnants.

Girls, no matter how equality-conscious their parents may be, all seem to go through a "Pink Phase," which can last for several years. During this time they yearn for a romantic pink haven in which to play their fairy-tale games, so be prepared to create a canopy emblazoned with draped pink organza or acquire some lace-trimmed bed linen. See page 83 for a pink room fit for a would-be princess.

There is no escaping the differences in behavior between girls and boys. A girl's Pink Phase is akin to the impulse that drives some boys, despite not being allowed to play with toy weapons, to create swords and rapiers from scrap pieces of cardboard and newspaper. Their heart's desire would be a room decked out as a pirate's cave or a sailboat, so steel yourself for time spent inserting eyelets into lengths of yacht canvas, lashing mock sails to bedposts, or decorating treasure chests.

Of course, there is no need to be so comprehensively indulgent when your child hits one of these phases. A generously draped bed canopy over a young girl's bed has been known to satisfy her romantic nature, while a temporary box of treasure and a passable cardboard imitation of a ship and a Jolly Roger flag could suffice for a boy.

Yet there is something incredibly satisfying about creating a complete scheme for a child's room. The distinct periods of childhood pass so quickly, and it is always the handmade beds and playhouses built over a weekend, the lovingly sewn quilts and dolls' house furnishings, or the personally stenciled toy boxes that children remember well into adulthood, and carry with them as talismans of their parents' affection.

These circus-style fabric-covered wardrobes add a touch of humor to striped walls and curtains. More stripes form tie-up shades on each wardrobe, while clowns adorn the wallpaper border and other small-scale detailing, making the circus theme complete. The buttoned heading on the curtains is echoed in the color of the drawer knobs.

FURNITURE, STORAGE, AND DISPLAY

In any bedroom, the bed is the most important piece of furniture you will acquire, and this is even more the case in children's rooms, as you want them to sleep comfortably and securely at night, with proper support for their backs.

In the early years, once a crib has been outgrown, at around the age of two, you should be able to combine the aesthetic with the practical and choose a bed to suit your circumstances. Antique box beds are perfect for the younger child as the sides are raised slightly at either end, preventing them from falling out in the night. Put wicker baskets under the bed for extra storage. Alternatively, contemporary pine beds often make use of the space under the mattress frame with generous-sized drawers on castors.

A pretty, draped four-poster bed is a lovely feature in this room decorated in simple pink and cream country florals. Delightfully feminine and irresistibly timeless, this rustic haven, with plum detailing and simple ruffles, is a fairy tale come true for girls of all ages.

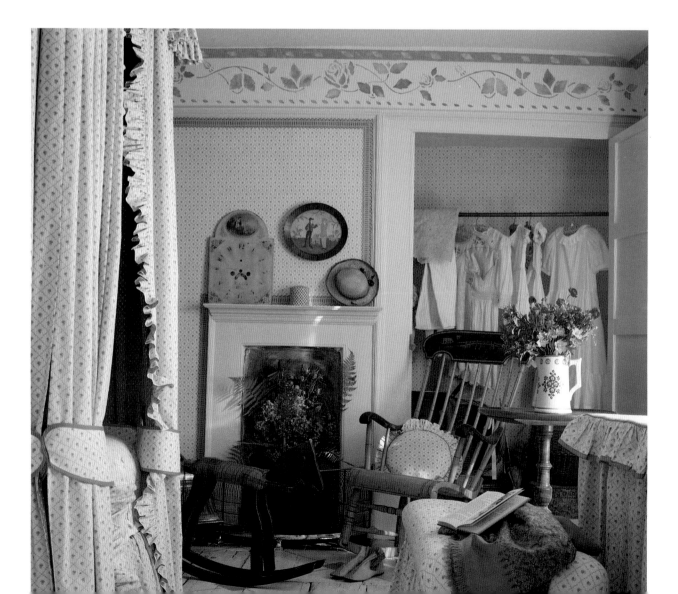

The most versatile of all beds are the bunk, platform, and loft beds, the components of which can be rearranged to form under-bed desks or shelves. Eminently practical and flexible, these components can be painted and distressed to make them look more appealing and in keeping with a traditional decorative scheme.

Beds also offer a good chance to reflect your chosen decorative theme with bed linen. Additional pillows, bolsters, or quilts in a style chosen by the children or parents can help unify or distinguish a particular theme. When pre-school children are going through the phase of wanting gaudy cartoon characters splashed over every movable object, it is usually acceptable to acquiesce on a couple of items, such as the pillowcase or duvet cover, on the understanding that a pretty bedcover adorns the bed for most of the day. Alternatively, stand your ground on bed linen, but be supremely indulgent when it comes to pajamas, nightdresses, and slippers!

Children's clothes and toys are often appealing decorative objects in their own right, so capitalize on this by showing them off to their full effect. Display baby clothes on small hangers suspended from peg rails, and intersperse them with rows of hats and hairbands or bags and puppets. Change the display regularly so that a baby has a varied view from the crib.

For all the other clothes and bed linen, the most useful pieces of furniture are a chest of drawers and, if there is no closet, a wardrobe or cupboard. A sturdy old pine chest will see a child right through from infancy to adulthood. Freestanding wardrobes are more versatile than built-in ones if you want to alter the room's layout when more children come along, or if you are marking the transition from one phase of childhood to the next. A row of built-in cupboards does make maximum use of space, however, and you can always consider replacing or painting the doors to add some variety.

Painted furniture is a real asset in children's rooms. Antique chests of drawers and bookshelves that have seen better days can be transformed with two coats of water-based paint in contrasting colors, their surfaces gently aged. For extra decoration, apply decoupage motifs or simple stencils to the finished pieces. For examples of this type of decoration on cupboards, furniture, and even a fireplace, see our Little Princess's Bedroom, page 84.

The more interesting and varied you can make the storage in a child's room, the more inclined they will be to help tidy up. It is much more appealing to help pile clothes into a colorful basket or a painted toy box than to cram objects into a battered cupboard or rows of junk-filled open shelves. Colorful baskets are also great for offsetting any garish plastic toys.

Screens are another useful way of disguising cluttered corners or partitioning a room when two children are sharing the same space. Use them to demarcate specific areas or as decorative objects in their own right. Paint them with blackboard paint, or coat them with a cork surface and use them as freestanding bulletin boards. Alternatively, cover them with fabric that matches the curtains and upholstery. You can also attach small hooks to the screens for displaying bags or for storing dressing-up clothes, creating an instant dressing room.

GETTING THE LIGHT RIGHT

Lighting is often ignored until the last moment when people are planning to decorate a room, but it is a vitally important element to get right. Children's rooms are no exception, and they call for a greater degree of flexibility and safety than other rooms in the house.

A dimmer switch for the main overhead light is the first requirement. From the nursery years onward, a dimmer is invaluable for providing just enough light to feed by, or if you want to check that children are tucked in nicely and fast asleep when you go to bed yourself.

Provide a wall-mounted lamp or bedside light for older children to read by, but do not leave any trailing cords visible. Lampshades, available in a wide variety of styles and colors for lamps and overhead pendant lights, are something children will enjoy choosing themselves. Plug-in nightlights are useful for nurseries, or for children who don't like complete darkness.

TRADITIONAL TOYS

Painted wooden toys will last a lifetime and offer a reassuring, nostalgic familiarity that can never be provided by mass-produced playthings. Nothing can match the timeless elegance of a polished and painted wooden rocking horse, a push-along puddleduck, a painted revolving merry-go-round, a set of weathered building blocks, or a well-loved dolls' house, whose smooth worn surfaces hint at the busy, happy hours of an earlier generation.

Children undoubtedly respond to bright primary colors, but they also appreciate natural textures, and the tactile qualities of wood and fabric surpass plastic every time. Painted wooden toys that can be handed down the generations make superb adornments for a child's room, so use them as decoration in their own right. Create a still life of wooden toys and soft rag dolls on a miniature wicker sofa, or line them up, two by two, atop a painted wall cupboard.

Another cherished possession of many children is the dressing-up box. Painted, stained, varnished, or stenciled, it is a treasure chest of props and clothes, hats and wraps, snakes and magic wands. The importance of creative play in a child's development is a favorite theme of child psychologists. Recent research suggests that an imaginative child is more likely to be receptive to learning and more able to take a balanced view of life's ups and downs.

Psychology apart, there is nothing quite so captivating as the sight of young children immersed in imaginative play. The sheer delight they take in transforming everyday objects into ever more complex and ornate props for their fantasy worlds is truly fascinating. Adults may be inspired by watching the way in which a bed, its duvet, blankets, and pillows can be transformed into glorious galleons or turreted castles. This kind of timeless make-believe is fun, free, and educational: the carpet might look like a utilitarian floor covering to you, but to children at play it becomes, with the addition of a few sofa cushions, a treacherous swamp inhabited by dangerous crocodiles. Only in a room in which children feel totally secure and comfortable can these forays into the imagination take place.

Encourage imaginative play by providing a few basic props such as floor pillows, discarded sheets with eyeholes cut out of them for ghost

This quintessential Victorian nursery incorporates subtle rose-colored fabric at the window and on the upholstery. A simple painted floor and a traditional rug are the perfect complements for traditional toys, such as a wooden rocking horse, dolls' house, and books.

and monster games, and a selection of hats for quick character changes. Don't forget that even everyday items like brooms, buckets, mops, and cardboard boxes can be put to good use by the would-be avenging swashbuckler or by the beautiful princess in peril.

CHAPTER TWO

Room for Change

Whapter you are planning a nursery for a new baby, it's difficult to think beyond the infant's immediate needs. The fact that a desk will be necessary at some remote time in the future seems hardly relevant when diaper-changing and feeding are dominating life.

Nevertheless, it's worth trying to think in the long-term. A little planning will allow you to adapt the room to the child's changing needs and interests without having to redecorate and refurnish completely. Not only is this approach more practical, but it will help maintain continuity through the years.

Wall and window treatments do not necessarily have to have a nursery motif to look appropriate for a baby. Instead, you can choose a design with a fairly broad appeal, then introduce the nursery element with pictures and accessories. Similarly, furniture can be adapted to different purposes over the years, as in the room featured on the following pages. It is shown in three guises: the first (left) is a nursery; the second (on page 27 and also shown in more detail in Chapter Four) is for a preschool child; and the third (on pages 28–29) is a teenager's room. The basics have remained the same, yet each room is both functional and appealing.

The first stage of our "transition room" shows a nursery configuration. The wallpaper border, with its Owl and the Pussycat theme, provided the starting point for the room. A thin strip of the border is repeated on the storage unit, while chambray blue, cowslip yellow, and apple green fabrics in checks and florals sit happily alongside colorwash-striped wallpaper. The generously draped Moses basket coordinates with the dresser unit, and a simply upholstered, sturdy chair will appeal to children of all ages.

INFANCY

The delightfully sunny scheme of sea blue and citrus yellow shown on pages 20–21 would suit either a girl or a boy. Checked curtains and striped wallpaper combine well with stenciled stars and moons taken from the wallpaper border. The shelves of the storage unit are lined with checked fabric, and a flat curtain covers the lower shelves; both fabrics match the colors of the florals used elsewhere in the room.

The multipurpose storage unit provides endlessly flexible accommodation for baby clothes and toiletries, as well as a diaper-changing area. Everything is at hand when the fold-down changing table is in use.

STORAGE UNIT

The freestanding storage unit, which serves as both a dresser and a changing table, consists of a shelf unit sitting on a base, both constructed from 1in (2.5cm) thick timber. The shelves on the base are made from slats attached to horizontal supports. A thick wooden dowel inserted through holes drilled in the frame provides hanging space for a baby's clothes. The dowel also extends beyond the shelves to act as a place to hang a handmade mobile (see page 26). The entire piece can be adjusted over the years to provide a variety of uses – as storage, work space, and hobby area (see page 31).

A changing table projects about 30in (75cm) at the side of the unit and has a wood support underneath. (Even though there is a rim around the edge, remember that a baby should never be left unattended on a changing table, however briefly, because of the risk of falling off.) The table can be folded down out of the way when not in use.

Brighten up the finished unit by lining the backs of the shelves on the top half with fabric, wallpaper, or wrapping paper. Decorate the rim with a narrow border; the one shown here was a detail taken from the Owl and the Pussycat wallpaper border that runs around the room at chair rail height. A coordinating fabric panel on the base unit conceals a useful storage area and softens the lines of the dresser. These finishing touches can all be altered at any time if you wish to change the look of the room.

LAYETTE BASKET

A basket like the one on the storage unit (opposite), with a pretty, washable lining, is indispensable in a nursery, and can be used in later years for storing all kinds of items.

YOU WILL NEED

FABRIC
MATCHING SEWING THREAD
LIGHTWEIGHT BATTING

1 Make a pattern and cut out fabric and batting for the base and sides, as directed for the Moses Basket Lining (page 44, step 1), but adding only ½in (1.25cm) all around for seam allowances.

2 Place the batting on the wrong side of one fabric piece for each side pattern; baste in place. Our lining is not quilted but you can quilt it if you wish (see page 45, Basket Lining step 2).

3 With right sides together, join both ends of the padded side pieces to form a ring, taking a ½in (1.25cm) seam. Trim away the batting in the seam allowances. Repeat for the unpadded fabric pieces.

4 Cut out 3in (7.5cm) wide strips for the ruffle and join the ends to make a single continuous strip that is double the distance around the rim. (Our fabric makes the ruffle appear to be cut on the bias, but it is cut on the straight grain.) Fold it in half lengthwise, wrong sides together; press and baste along the long raw edge. Arrange the folded strip into ½in (1.25cm) knife pleats every 1¾in (4.5cm) or so. Baste along the raw edge of the ruffle.

5 Make four pairs of ties by cutting eight 2in (5cm) wide fabric strips on the straight grain; they should be long enough to tie in bows around the basket handles. Fold each in half lengthwise, right sides together, and stitch down the long edge, taking a ¼in (6mm) seam, and then stitch across one end at an angle. Trim the corners, turn right side out, and press.

6 Position the pleated ruffle along the top edge of the padded ring, right sides together and raw edges even; baste in place. Place two ties, one over the other, on top of the ruffle, with raw edges even, positioning them on one side of the handle. Do the same with two more on the other side of the handle. Repeat for the handle at the other end of the ring.

7 Lay the other ring on top, right sides together, and stitch around the top edge, taking a ½in (1.25cm) seam, and sandwiching in the ruffle and the ties. Trim seam, clip curves, and trim away the batting within the seam allowances. Turn right side out. Press, then baste the layers together along the lower edge.

8 Join the lower edge of the ring to the base (see page 45, Basket Lining step 4). Place the lining in the basket, and tie to the handles.

MOSES BASKET SKIRT AND CANOPY

A pleated skirt covers the stand of this Moses basket. The box pleats are arranged so that the checked bands of the fabric fall inside the pleats. The basket lining is made from the coordinating check fabric and trimmed with a plain fabric that picks out the blue found in the fabrics and elsewhere in the room. Above the basket a simple voile canopy is suspended from a wall-mounted pole. (This canopy should not be used when a baby is old enough to pull on it.)

YOU WILL NEED

FOR SKIRT AND QUILT
FLORAL FABRIC FOR SKIRT AND QUILT
CHECKED FABRIC FOR BASKET LINING AND RUFFLE ON QUILT
PLAIN FABRIC FOR TRIM
MATCHING SEWING THREAD
MEDIUM-WEIGHT BATTING

FOR CANOPY
BLOCK OF WOOD ½IN (1.25CM) THICK AND ABOUT 4IN (10CM) SQUARE
10IN (25CM) LENGTH OF WOODEN DOWELLING
VOILE OR MUSLIN
MATCHING SEWING THREAD

Skirt and quilt

1 From the checked fabric, make the lining as for the Layette Basket (page 23), steps 1–3.

2 Measure the distance from the top of the basket to the floor. Cut pieces of fabric to this length plus 1¾in (4.5cm) and join together at the sides until you have a ring measuring twice the distance around the basket. Press under ¼in (6mm) and then 1in (2.5cm) on the lower edge, and stitch. Arrange the fabric in equal box pleats so that the ring fits exactly around the top of the basket. If you are using the fabric we used, the checked bands should fall inside the pleats. Baste all around.

3 Cut 3in (7.5cm) wide strips of plain fabric on the bias and join the ends (page 89, step 4) to form a continuous ring long enough to fit around the top of the pleated skirt. Lay it on the top and mark where the handles will be. Make an opening like a bound buttonhole large enough for each handle.

4 With right sides together, sew one edge of the trim to the top of the pleated skirt, and the other to the top of the padded lining. Complete as for the Layette Basket (page 23), steps 7–8, slotting the buttonholes over the handles rather than tying the lining in place as for the Layette Basket.

5 Make the quilt from the floral fabric, as for the quilt on page 45, inserting a wide checked ruffle in the outer seam.

Canopy

1 Cut a ½in (1.25cm) thick block of wood into the shape shown. Drill a hole in it the same diameter as, or slightly less than, the dowel. Screw the block to the wall about 6ft (1.8m) above floor level, using several screws. Shave the end of the dowel with a knife if necessary so it will fit tightly into the hole in the wood block.

2 Cut a 14ft (4.3m) length of voile and hem the ends. (Using the full width of fabric eliminates the need for hems on the side edges.) Fold in half crosswise, right sides together, and stitch ½in (1.25cm) from the fold to form a casing. Turn over, slot the dowel through the casing, and drape around the basket.

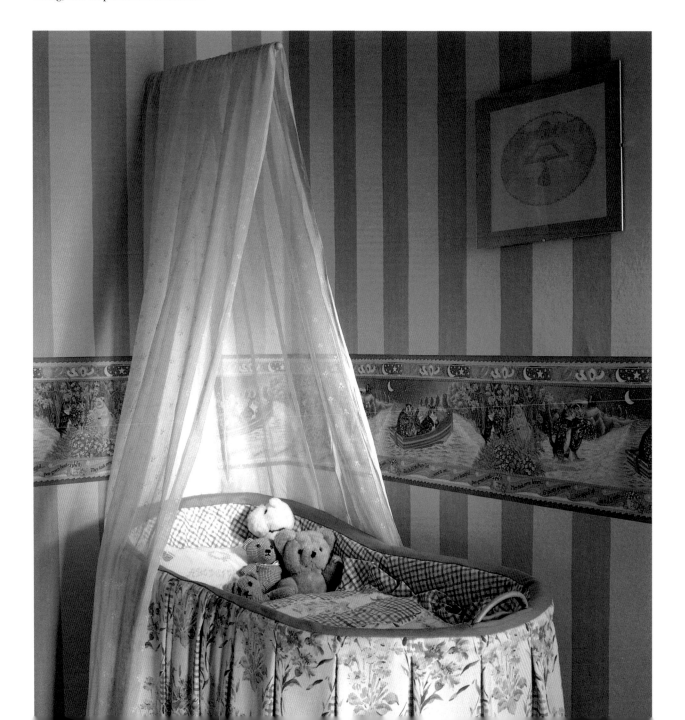

MOBILE

All the elements of this fabric mobile are taken from the Owl and the Pussycat rhyme that appears on the wallpaper border: the owl's guitar, the "honey and plenty of money, wrapped up in a five-pound note," the stars they looked up to, the moon whose light they danced by, and especially the ring that enabled the pair to marry after sailing away for a year and a day.

YOU WILL NEED

2 PLASTIC-COATED WIRE COATHANGERS
THICK COTTON THREAD
FABRIC FOR COVERING HANGER
FELT FOR SHAPES
MATCHING SEWING THREAD
GINGHAM FOR HONEYPOT
CORD FOR HONEYPOT
BATTING
SMALL COINS, TO USE AS WEIGHTS

1 Squeeze the top and bottom of each coathanger together. Insert one hanger through the other with the two hooks together and twist the hangers into a four-pointed star. Wrap thick cotton thread around the center.

2 Cut five 3in (7.5cm) wide strips of fabric, each 1½ times the length of an "arm" of the star. Fold in half length-wise, right sides together, and stitch along the long edge and across one end. Turn right side out. Run a gathering thread along the length of each and pull up the threads. Encase the arms and also the hook in these gathered fabric tubes. Turn under the raw ends and hand sew the tubes together at the center.

3 Cut out two shapes from the felt for each item. Machine stitch the smaller shapes onto each side. Machine stitch the guitar strings and fret in brown, and zigzag stitch the numeral "5" on the five-pound note. Stitch the two layers of each together around the edges, inserting a little batting between the layers first. For the stars and guitar you could also insert a small coin as a weight. For the honeypot, add a gingham lid, trimmed with cord.

4 Suspend the felt pieces from the arms of the star with thick cotton thread, adjusting the lengths of the thread and the positions of the pieces so that the mobile looks balanced. If you want the mobile to move a lot, the lengths of string will need to be longer than those in the photograph.

PRESCHOOL

When adapting the nursery to suit a preschool child, the wallpaper, the stenciled stars and moons, and the checked curtains can all stay as they are, and the storage unit can now be used for keeping toys tidy. A crib or a bed replaces the original Moses basket or cradle, and the fabric that was chosen for the Moses basket and nursery dresser is suitable for a duvet cover and pillowcase. The wallpaper border that appeared at chair rail height in the nursery is featured again, around the bottom of the bed this time.

Space has been left on the floor for lots of toys and for a foldaway playhouse, which is an ideal plaything for children of this age. Foldaway items allow you to clear the decks at the end of a day's play so that the toys do not lose their novelty value.

Any additional storage requirements can be accommodated by adding a fabric-covered wardrobe (see page 56). One of the advantages of this sort of storage is that it provides another opportunity to introduce fabric, which can be changed, if desired, when the child is older. (For more about this room, see page 52.)

In the second stage of our "transition room," the former nursery has been adapted for a preschool child. The basics — wallpaper and stenciled frieze, curtains and flooring — are still the same, but a fun four-poster bed now has pride of place. The entire room is described in detail and illustrated on pages 52–57.

THE TEENS

When a tiny baby has become an active teenager, with study, relaxation, and entertaining as the main priorities, the room is again easily adapted to a new age group. The original dresser storage unit now becomes a desk, providing a quiet and useful study area.

The wallpaper and curtains remain, but new bedspreads have been added for the full-size bed and for a mattress used as a low day bed, and there are now some soft, squashy accent pillows. Scraps of the existing fabrics have been incorporated in an oversized bedspread made from a matching blue fabric and edged in a wide border of ticking stripes. They help to unite the existing decor and the new approach. The pillows have a variety of borders and edgings, while the day bed is draped in a patchwork quilt of florals and checks. The original dressing-up box of several years ago is now an impromptu coffee table.

The atmosphere of the room is totally different from that of the nursery on pages 20–21, yet many of the original features are still in evidence. Careful planning of a child's room at the outset can pay dividends for years to come. Your teenager may also be secretly pleased that some vestigial elements of childhood remain.

A colorful retreat, this cool chambray blue, cowslip yellow, and apple green room – the third stage of our "transition room" – is both comfortable and inspiring for a busy teenager. With plenty of space to relax with friends, as well as a comfortable worktop, a desk, and ample space for a bulletin board, emphasis is placed on the dramatic combination of checks and stripes in the three main colors.

29

APPLIQUÉD PATCH BEDSPREAD

The patches on this upbeat bedspread are not pieced but appliquéd onto the background fabric. Cut bold patches in a range of shapes, sizes, and fabrics, and appliqué them by turning under a narrow hem then hand sewing all around each edge. The large embroidery stitches used around the edges of the patches are in keeping with the bold design. Blanket stitches worked along the inner edge of the striped border help frame the patches and unify the designs. This is a project an artistic teenager might like to help with.

PILLOWS

Piles of pillows are often considered essential in a teenager's room. Make them from fabrics used elsewhere in the room, and add variety with the trim. The measurements given here are for 24in (60cm) square cushions, but they can be adjusted easily.

YOU WILL NEED

FABRIC

MATCHING THREAD

PIPING CORD AND BIAS BINDING IN CONTRASTING FABRIC, FOR PIPED PILLOWS

COVERED BUTTONS, FOR BUTTONED PILLOW

24IN (60CM) PILLOW FORMS

Flanged pillow

1 For a pillow that has a 4in (10cm) flange all around, cut a 25 x 25in (63.5 x 63.5cm) square, one 25 x 31in (63.5 x 79cm) rectangle, and four 33 x 9in (84 x 23cm) strips of fabric. Cut the rectangle in half crosswise and turn under ¼in (6mm) then 1in (2.5cm) on the cut edge of both halves.

2 With *wrong* sides together and raw edges even, pin the back pieces to the front piece, overlapping the hemmed edges at the back to create an opening. Baste all around.

3 Press under ½in (1.25cm) on one long edge of each strip. With right sides together, stitch the other edge of each strip to the basted edges of the fabric squares, taking a ½in (1.25cm) seam and stopping at the seamlines of the adjacent edges. Miter the corners as shown. Turn each strip to the other side, pin the folded edge along the seamline, and stitch along the seamline. Press. Insert the pillow form through the opening in the back.

Buttoned pillow

1 Cut a 25 x 31in (63.5 x 79cm) rectangle for the front and a 25 x 25in (63.5 x 63.5cm) square for the back. Mark a line 6in (15cm) in from one short edge of the rectangle, and cut along this line.

2 Turn under ¼in (6mm) and then 1in (2.5cm) on the cut edges of the two front pieces, and make buttonholes in the narrower piece.

3 Place the front and back pieces with right sides together, raw edges even, and the hemmed edges overlapping so that the narrower front piece is next to the back piece. Stitch a ½in (1.25cm) seam around all four sides. Trim the corners and turn right side out. Sew

covered buttons onto the wider front piece, beneath the buttonholes.

Piped pillow

Make an opening in the back as for the flanged pillow, but join the front and back with *right* sides together, inserting piping in the seam (see page 89, step 5). To make bias binding for the piping, see page 89, step 4.

STORAGE UNIT

The baby's dresser (page 22) is easily transformed into a study area with plenty of accessible storage. The fold-down table has been turned over so that it can be used as a desk; the rim that was on the changing table is now part of the decorative edging. The curtain panel that was on the base unit has been removed, revealing the slatted shelves, and the original fabric backing on the top unit has been replaced with wrapping paper. Providing capacious but accessible storage, as well as a good-sized tabletop, the unit is as invaluable in a teenager's room as in that of a newborn babe.

CHAPTER THREE

The Nursery Years

A few centuries ago, nursery folklore demanded that a newborn baby be held aloft as soon as it was born, to insure that it would do well and rise in the world. These days, a colorful, stimulating environment in which to spend time and play is recognized as a prerequisite for a happy, healthy child. As a result, the decoration and planning of a first nursery has become a priority.

The notion of a traditional nursery, with its draped wooden crib, pristine white bedding, and lovingly sewn quilts, is tremendously appealing. The magical presence of a peacefully sleeping baby never fails to touch all generations as they marvel over its delicate features and tiny fingers.

Harness some of the wonder of a new baby by making the nursery a place where the new family member can thrive and develop in surroundings that inspire and delight. Fill it with special family heirlooms such as hand-embroidered birth samplers and weathered wooden baby carriages, old blanket boxes, or treasured teddy bears, and simple soft toys. Such timeless items will easily make the transition from one period of childhood to the next.

Our Ducks Nursery (see page 39) features a modern interpretation of traditional animal motifs. Ducks and the color yellow are both classic choices for a nursery because they suit boys *and* girls. Yellow checked curtains are neatly pinned back with a yellow tieback finished off with a blue gingham covered button. The gingham is echoed in the wall hanging.

CHOOSING THE PLACE

Try to place a nursery at the back of the home, away from street noise, and preferably in a room that receives a fair amount of natural light during the day – a southern exposure is ideal.

When choosing which room of the house to devote to the nursery, it isn't always entirely practical to do as the Victorians did and select the smallest room at the top of the house. In the first year of your baby's life, you will be backward and forward to the nursery countless times, and the rest of the time you'll be listening for the baby, so try not to have too much distance between the nursery and your bedroom.

Babies grow so quickly that by the age of about two, a child will require a full-size single bed, additional toy and clothes storage, and a clear floor space for playing. By thinking ahead at the very beginning you should be able to work out which will be the most suitable room for adapting from a cute, minimally furnished nursery, to a virtual toy store, to a place for slumber parties, to a teenage den.

It may be worth putting the nursery in the smallest bedroom if it is next to an existing bedroom. You could then consider turning the two rooms into one when the baby is old enough to share a room with an older sibling. Alternatively, think about devoting a larger bedroom (yours perhaps) to a room that will double up as bedroom and playroom for years to come, thereby keeping space elsewhere free for the grown-ups.

CREATING A NURSERY

The decorating and equipping of a nursery is an exciting departure into the hitherto mysterious world of cribs, musical mobiles, and wallpaper borders, as well as an important chance to prepare yourself for a new way of life.

With the imminent arrival of a new baby, particularly the first one, there is a strong temptation to create a special room festooned in yards of soft-colored delicate fabrics, with every available surface emblazoned with stenciled motifs. While such a tailor-made room is idyllic for a baby up to 12 months old, it quickly becomes inappropriate thereafter. A little restraint and a careful use of color, fabric, and furniture at an early stage will enable you to lay the decorative foundations of a room that has to evolve through several different stages of childhood.

Decorating a nursery provides a rare opportunity to plan and style a room from scratch as well as a chance to be more adventurous with color and pattern than you might be in a formal living room or in a much-viewed kitchen. You can decide for yourself exactly what colors to use, choose very specific fabrics, and unleash your artistic yearnings by decorating old chests of drawers or creating crib quilts and wall hangings.

Whether you settle on a cohesive scheme in which coordinating fabrics appear on curtains, upholstery, lampshades, and accessories, or an eclectic mix of colors and patterns, there are a few basic guidelines to make your life easier when planning the decor.

DECORATING

Very often it is the window treatment that triggers ideas for how to use fabric elsewhere in the room. A simple shade calls for a simple crib duvet, while a curtain valance and tiebacks could suggest a crib or bed canopy in another part of the room. Equally, plain, lined pencil pleat curtains in a beautiful fabric offer simple, classic comfort and warmth.

Wallpaper borders are often good starting points for decorative schemes too. They usually incorporate a wide range of colors, any of which can be picked out and emphasized in wall color, curtain fabric, cradle or crib linen, and upholstery. A bold border could be echoed with equally bold pillows in the dominant color but toned down with simple checked curtains. Similarly, checked curtains could be contrasted with striped or polkadotted designs in the same colors used on small-scale accessories such as floor pillows and laundry bags. Mixing quite different fabrics in this way can be very successful and create surprising contrasts.

The nursery is the perfect chance to use animal motifs, which are nearly as popular with adults as with children. Themes such as the circus, nursery rhymes, teddy bears, numbers, and the alphabet also have a timeless appeal.

A predominately pink or blue nursery is fine if you know in advance the sex of your child, or if you are prepared to postpone decorating the nursery till after the birth. Specifically feminine and masculine rooms can be created not just with color but also with fabric – florals for girls and stripes for boys.

A procession of white farmyard ducks in a field of yellow daffodils makes a beautiful wallpaper border, especially painted in watercolors. The border was the starting point for the scheme for the Ducks Nursery (page 38).

Many nurseries, or course, are decorated before the baby's sex is known. Checks are a popular design for both boys and girls and work well with the "unisex" colors of green, yellow, and red. Our simple yellow Ducks Nursery (pages 32–33) with checked curtains and a duck-motif wallpaper border (page 35) suits baby boys and girls. The classic nursery combination of green and yellow or blue and yellow also works for either sex. You can always add small accessories such as mobiles and posters in a defining color if you wish. Another option is to paint the walls white or cream and choose a wall-paper border, but leave the choice of curtains and crib linen until after the birth.

Since babies spend quite a lot of time in their cribs, consider painting small motifs – stars and moons or simple shapes – onto the ceiling. Or use a strong color on the ceiling if the room is quite a good size. (Avoid deep colors in a small or low-ceilinged room, as it will make it seem even smaller.)

Floorboards look pretty stenciled with simple flowers or geometric shapes, or simply glazed in white or bright colors. Set them off with a large rag rug in the center.

Although it is tempting to use ruffled or fussy curtains at the windows, often a more restrained look works better – and is easier to adapt later on. Try ungathered lengths of fabric lashed to metal or wooden poles by means of punched eyelets and thick jute rope, or simple Roman or roller shades embellished with contrasting plain fabric edges or pulls.

EQUIPPING A NURSERY

Regardless of the style of decor you are planning, there is a certain amount of essential equipment for which you will need to find space (see opposite). The ideal nursery will be large enough to house a single bed eventually. It should have a decent-sized window and adequate heating and lighting. If possible, it should include a sink and a storage unit, which is invaluable at nighttime during the months of frequent diaper-changing.

Essential furniture includes a cradle or crib and adequate storage. Built-in cupboards are useful for storing clothes, diapers and creams, and spare towels and bedding, while babies' clothes are easily stored in drawers or on shelves.

A diaper-changing area will prevent backache if you are using a changing pad and constantly bending down to the floor. Fabric wall pockets set at the appropriate height are useful for storing the most frequently used changing equipment while keeping the room clutter-free. (See page 80 for full instructions on how to make these.) Or fix castors to an old lidded box and store the diaper paraphernalia in it as a mobile changing unit.

A cupboard or wardrobe with doors will contain clothes that are still too big or already outgrown. Freestanding wardrobes or children's-size clothes rails are more versatile than a built-in system, unless it is tailor-made for children and designed to be upgraded at a later date. An easy chair for comfortable feeding is also a must. A low, fairly upright, armless chair is usually recommended, though you may prefer one that has arms, so you can rest your elbows while feeding. If it is an old chair from another part of the house, cover it with a throw that works with the other colors in the room. A side table with a small light is also useful for resting books and a baby's drinks on.

It is a good idea to provide some sort of miniature seating. In the early days it can be used for displaying the soft toys new babies are inevitably showered with. Seating can take the form of small wicker chairs, sofas with lift-up seats, little cane chairs, tiny upholstered chairs, or small wooden stools and benches.

Baskets in vibrant colors that blend in with your scheme are ideal for babies' rooms. Buy several in a variety of sizes, and use them for laundry or toys or simply for decoration. Between the ages of 12 and 18 months, babies adore emptying and filling baskets with all kind of objects, so keep a small basket of toys in the kitchen, bathroom, and living room, or any other room your child regularly follows you into.

It is never too early to invest in an old blanket box or a toy trunk for storing bits and pieces. It will be used for many years to come, for everything from toys and sports equipment to spare bedding and, if it has a lock, a teenager's secret letters and keepsakes.

Slumbering teddies prove that comfortable pillows and bedding in soft colors, punctuated with delicate bows, deep ruffles, and fringed trimmings, do much to create an atmosphere of relaxation.

THE NURSERY:
FURNISHING SUGGESTIONS

Moses basket, cradle, or carrycot
Crib and mattress
Crib bumper
Cradle and crib sheets
Cradle and crib blankets
Crib quilt (do not use a pillow during a baby's first year)
Baby bath or bath insert
Changing pad
Chest of drawers
Comfortable chair
Small side table and light
Storage for toys or bed linen
Mobiles
Small chairs or stools

DETAILS

In many ways, the busier-looking a nursery, the better. Babies love color and movement, so fix a musical mobile onto the crib, or above it, and a couple of other mobiles nearby. Put one near a doorway or window so any slight breeze or ray of light will cause it to twinkle and shimmer. Make your own mobiles from simple felt shapes, dismantled and painted egg cartons adorned with metallic paper flags, or tiny bells attached to wooden balls pierced with fine florists' wire. Always make sure that mobiles are fixed securely and there is no danger of their falling or being pulled into the cradle or crib, or of pieces coming off that the baby could swallow.

Try to think of the nursery from a baby's viewpoint. A pleasing tableau is of little use if it is too high up on a wall. It may look good to an adult walking into the room, but the baby will not be able to see it at all.

Peg rails or metal coat hooks are versatile additions to a nursery, allowing you to store and display clothes at the same time. Wax, stain, or paint individual rails and arrange them in a continuous line or in twos or threes around the room. Use coathangers that blend with your theme – these could be padded hangers decorated with a delicate lace border, or painted wooden shapes such as clowns' heads.

For the walls, buy sheets of charming children's wrapping paper or colorful wallpapers or borders featuring the alphabet, numbers, or animal illustrations and place them in simple clip frames. Change or rearrange them regularly to provide variety.

Make a display feature of heirloom china, porcelain dolls, or well-loved old teddy bears in an antique glass-fronted display case mounted on the wall. Or create a faux dresser by fixing an old shallow bookcase against the wall to rest on top of a small chest of drawers. Strip or paint the pieces to match and display rag dolls, teddies, and wooden toys on them.

THE DUCKS NURSERY

Animals are ideal starting points for decorating a nursery. The duck theme of our nursery (shown on pages 32–33) is neither too masculine nor too feminine, often an advantage if you want to decorate in advance of a new arrival. For the same reason, the yellow used on the walls and curtains is a sensible color to choose. It is also extremely versatile, working equally well in small, dark rooms or in large, light rooms.

The duck theme emerged from the colorful wallpaper border that runs around the room at chair rail height. This particular border was chosen not only because ducks are so popular with children but also because it would quite happily make the transition from nursery to preschool child's room. Like the theme itself, the colors of the border – a combination of green, blue, and yellow – are suitable for boys or girls.

Repeating a motif from your fabric or furnishings as a decorative device on doors, covered boxes, walls, or furniture is a good way to unify a scheme. You can make it as subtle or as obvious as your taste dictates. Here, we cut out the animal motifs from a length of coordinating fabric and used them repeatedly on a patchwork crib quilt.

The duck motifs are also used on both sides of the cupboard doors in the nursery. To keep the design simple, they are outlined in a heavy pencil line then colored-in with watered-down paint for a pale, muted effect. On the back wall of the cupboard they are echoed with solid-yellow ducks applied with a stencil.

To transfer a drawing to a surface such as a stencil or cupboard door, first trace your motif from the wallpaper or border frieze onto tracing paper (you can enlarge or reduce an image with a photocopier or by using graph paper). Transfer it to the stencil card or to the cupboard door using carbon paper or by drawing the image on the reverse side of the tracing paper with a very soft pencil then laying the penciled side against the surface and drawing or rubbing over the outlines from the front of the paper.

The duck motif used in the nursery is here repeated inside a cupboard. On the inside of the door, the ducks are painted freehand, while they are stenciled onto the wall at the back.

PATCHWORK CRIB QUILT OR PLAY MAT

A quilt or, later on, duvet cover, properly made of pure, crisp cotton in appealing colors, will become a treasured family heirloom to pass on to future generations. A quilt is at once useful, decorative, and lasting – a treasured possession.

Quilts have a long and fascinating history and vary widely in design. Although many beautiful quilts are produced using only a single piece of fabric on top, it is patchwork that is most closely associated with quilting. Originally a thrifty method employed by country folk as a means of keeping warm in the winter, it has become virtually an art form in itself.

These days, machine-patchwork quilts are just as pleasing as labor-intensive handmade quilts, and offer a time-saving way of creating something special for the nursery. With the addition of appliqué motifs or images, these quilts are frequently decorative enough to hang on the wall.

This crib quilt – which can also double as a play mat – incorporates fabric that coordinates with the wallpaper border, plus simple checks and stripes in colors that echo the walls and curtains. Using two checked, one striped, and one patterned fabric, as here, you can make an endless variety of patterns from patchwork squares. Choose fabrics and batting that are all washable.

MEASURING

These instructions are for a quilt measuring 46 x 30in (117 x 76cm). It is made up of 15 blocks, each 8in (20cm) square, arranged in five rows of three blocks each, surrounded by a 4in (10cm) border. The unquilted dimensions are 48 x 32in (122 x 81cm); the quilting, however, makes it "shrink" a little. For the quilt to fit your crib exactly, it may be necessary to adjust the size of the blocks or border, or to alter the number of blocks.

YOU WILL NEED

FABRIC: SMALL CHECK, LARGE CHECK, STRIPE, DUCK PRINT, AND PLAIN
MATCHING SEWING THREAD
MEDIUM-WEIGHT BATTING

1 From the duck fabric, cut out eight 9in (22.5cm) squares of fabric on the straight grain, each bearing a duck motif. From the small check, cut out one 9in (22.5cm) square on the diagonal and ten 5in (12.5cm) squares on the straight grain. From the striped fabric, cut out eight 5in (12.5cm) squares, four of them on the straight grain and four on the diagonal. Also from this fabric cut out eight 3 x 9in (7.5 x 22.5cm) rectangles.

2 With right sides together and raw edges even, join a checked square to a striped square, taking a ½in (1.25cm) seam. Repeat, then join the two pairs of squares to make one block. Make three more blocks of checked and striped squares in the same way. Press.

3 Again with right sides together and raw edges even, join a striped rectangle to one side of a checked square, taking a ½in (1.25cm) seam, starting and stopping ½in (1.25cm) in from each end. Stitch striped rectangles to the other three edges in the same way. Press. Miter each corner by stitching with right sides together from the end of the stitching to the outside edge on the diagonal, as shown. Press.

4 Arrange the patches as shown in the photograph and stitch them together into rows, right sides together and taking ½in (1.25cm) seams. Press. Now stitch the rows together, taking care to match the seams.

5 From the small check, cut out four 3in (7.5cm) wide strips on the straight grain. Two of the strips should be the width of the patchwork portion, and the other two should be the length of the patchwork portion plus 5in (12.5cm). With right sides together and taking a ½in (1.25cm) seam, stitch a short strip to each end of the patchwork. In the same way, stitch a long strip to each side, so that the ends of the long strips are flush with the edges of the short strips. Press.

6 From the plain fabric, cut out four 2½in (6.5cm) wide strips on the straight grain. Two of the strips should be as long as the width of the quilt including the checked border, and two should be as long as the length of the quilt including the checked border. Fold one short strip in half lengthwise, wrong sides together, and lay it on top of the checked border at one end, with raw edges even. Stitch through all three thicknesses, taking a ½in (1.25cm) seam, and starting and stopping ½in (1.25cm) from the ends.

7 Fold the other strips in half lengthwise in the same way. Stitch the remaining short strip to the other end, and stitch the two long strips to the sides, again starting and stopping ½in (1.25cm) from the ends. Miter the corners as in step 3. Press. For now, leave the plain border facing inward, with the raw edges on the outside

8 From the large-check fabric, cut a 53 x 37in (135 x 94cm) rectangle on the straight grain. From the batting cut a 48 x 32in (122 x 81cm) rectangle.

9 Lay the large-check rectangle wrong side up on a flat surface and center the batting on top of it. Lay the patchwork right side up, centered on top of the batting. Baste the quilt together through all layers around the outer edges and alongside the seams between blocks, starting at the center of the quilt and working outward so that the fabric will be flat and smooth. Quilt by machine-stitching around the edges of

the blocks through all layers. Remove the basting.

10 Turn under and press ½in (1.25cm) along the raw edges of the backing fabric and bring it over to the front, so the folded edge is even with the outer seamline. Stitch all around, along the edge. To miter each corner, turn in the corner and trim off the point before folding the straight edges forward.

11 Turn the green border to the outside so it overlaps the large-check border, and topstitch along the inner edge through all layers.

DUCKS AND FLOWERS WALL HANGING

YOU WILL NEED

FABRIC: PLAIN AND CHECK

MATCHING SEWING THREAD

FELT: WHITE, ORANGE, TWO SHADES OF
YELLOW, BLACK

WHITE CRAFT GLUE

NARROW DOWEL

The bold, naive style of fabric wall hangings makes them ideal for the nursery, particularly when they are large and colorful. This simple one has been designed to blend in with the nursery duck theme, but any simple motifs can be used. Position the hanging so your baby is able to see it from the crib, and move it around the room from time to time to provide variety. See the templates at the back of the book for a selection of duck templates.

1 Cut out a rectangle of plain fabric to the desired size, adding ½in (1.25cm) all around for seam allowances. For the border cut two strips of checked fabric, on the straight grain, to the desired width – say, 4in (10cm) – plus 1in (2.5cm) for seam allowances, by the depth of the plain rectangle. Cut two more strips to the same width, by the width of the picture plus twice the width of the strip itself.

2 With right sides together and raw edges even, stitch the two shorter strips to the sides of the plain rectangle, taking a ½in (1.25cm) seam. Turn the borders to the right side and press. Stitch the other two strips to the top and bottom in the same way, with the ends flush with the side edges of the shorter strips. Turn to the right side and press.

3 For the hanging loops, cut a 16 x 2in (40.5 x 5cm) length of checked fabric on the straight grain. Fold the long edges so they meet in the center, then fold in half lengthwise; press and stitch. Cut into four equal lengths. Fold each one in half crosswise and place along the top edge of the hanging, on the right side. Position them so that the raw ends are at the top edge, and so that they are spaced equally across the hanging. Baste the loops in place.

4 Cut a backing piece from the checked fabric, making it the same size as the front of the hanging. Position it on top of the other piece, right sides together. Stitch all around the edges

taking a ½in (1.25cm) seam and leaving a 6in (15cm) opening at the top of the seam on one side of the hanging. Trim the corners, turn right side out, and press. Insert the dowel through the opening and hand sew it in place inside the wall hanging at the top.

5 Using the templates at the back of the book, and reducing or enlarging them as necessary, cut out the duck shapes from felt. Use white felt for the body and wing, orange for the feet and beak, and black for the eye of each duck. Glue these to the wall hanging using the photograph as a guide.

6 For each daffodil, cut out the six-petaled flower from felt in the lighter yellow and the circular center from the slightly deeper yellow. Cut out small

Vs all around the edge of the center. Glue in place.

For each daisy, cut a white circle, snip it irregularly around the edge, and fan it out to make the shape slightly concave before sticking the center to the fabric. Cut out a small orange circle and glue it in the middle of the white circle. Suspend the hanging from four small nails using the loops.

BUTTON-TRIMMED VALANCE

This elegant valance, incorporating classic pinch pleats decorated with fabric-covered buttons, is a stylish solution for a nursery. Simple curtains can be made to appear much more special with the addition of a coordinating valance and tie-backs. Here, the plain fabric valance, which is accompanied by matching tiebacks, continues the yellow color theme of the nursery. The tiebacks and the pinch pleats of the valance are decorated with buttons covered in the blue gingham used for the border of the wall hanging and for the Moses basket edging and quilt.

MOSES BASKET LINING AND QUILT

For the first two or three months of life, babies love the comfort and security provided by a snugly padded Moses basket. Lightly covered but protected by the high fabric-decorated sides of a soft carrying basket, they will sleep all the better. This basket has padded sides and a simple matching quilt.

Making the lining pattern

To insure a perfect fit for your own basket, you will need to make a paper pattern from brown paper or newspaper. First make a pattern for the base. Inside the basket, cover the base with paper and run your fingers or scissors handles around the sides, then trim to shape. Label the top and bottom ends. Put this in place while you make the pattern for the sides.

Baskets are rarely symmetrical, so you'll need to make a pattern to go all the way around. Cut a rectangle to fit roughly around the top half and another for the bottom half, so they meet in the middle. Cut about six slits at regular intervals in each rectangle from the top almost to the bottom, so that each slit opens up to help the paper fit around the curving sides. Fill in the triangular space in each split with paper, sticking it in place with transparent tape. Trim the top edge to ½in (1.25cm) below the top of the basket. You will now have two pieces shaped rather like fat boomerangs. Label which is the top half and which the bottom half.

Basket lining

1 Use your base pattern to cut out one piece of main fabric for the base, adding ½in (1.25cm) all around for seam allowances. Fold the fabric in half and use each side pattern to cut two pieces of fabric on the bias, adding 1in (2.5cm) all around for seam allowances and for a "shrinkage" allowance caused by the quilting. For the edging, cut an 8½in (22.5cm) wide strip of contrasting fabric on the bias, making it long enough to fit all around the top plus 1in (2.5cm) for seams. Cut one piece of batting for each half of the sides, the same size as the fabric pieces, and cut a 4in (10cm) wide strip of batting the same length as the fabric piece for the edging.

2 Sandwich one piece of batting between the two corresponding fabric pieces, right sides on the outside, and baste together all over by hand. Quilt by machine-stitching lines about 2¾in (7cm) apart in a grid pattern, using the check pattern as guide lines. Repeat for the other side piece.

3 With right sides together and raw edges even, stitch the two padded pieces together at both ends to form a ring, taking ½in (1.25cm) seams. Trim away the batting within the seam allowances. Check that the padded ring fits inside the basket exactly, and adjust if necessary.

4 With right sides together and raw edges even, join the lower edges of the ring to the base, taking a ½in (1.25cm) seam. Trim away the batting within the seam allowance, and clip the curves. Check again that it fits.

5 Baste the long strip of batting to the wrong side of the strip of contrasting fabric along one long side, so the raw edges are even on that side. With right sides together and raw edges even, stitch the padded fabric strip around the top edge of the lining, taking a ½in (1.25cm) seam. Trim away the batting

within the seam allowance. Wrap the other half of the strip over the batting, turn under ½in (1.25cm) and slipstitch to the outside.

6 Make six machine buttonholes near the folded edge of this padded strip, positioning one in the center of each side and spacing the others equally. Cover the button forms with the main fabric, following the manufacturer's directions, and attach these to the outside of the basket in line with the buttonholes using a needle and thread. Insert the lining in the basket, and button in place.

Quilt

1 Cut out two rectangular pieces from the contrasting fabric, each measuring the width of the basket plus 8in (20.5cm) by the length of the basket plus 2in (5cm). Cut off the bottom corners in a continuous curve to fit. Cut one piece of batting to this size.

2 Sandwich the batting between the two layers of fabric, and baste together. Machine quilt on a 5in (12.5cm) diagonal grid. Remove basting.

3 Cut 3in (8cm) wide strips of the same fabric on the bias. Join the ends of the strips together to make enough bias binding to go around the quilt (see page 89, step 4). Turn under and press ¼in (6mm) along both raw edges, then fold the strip in half lengthwise, wrong sides together. Wrap the binding over the raw edges of the quilt to enclose them. Pin and then baste in place all around. Stitch through all layers; remove basting.

CHAPTER FOUR

The Preschool Years

The watershed between infancy and the preschool years seems to occur at around the time when children need their first proper bed. From now on, individual personalities emerge as their specific likes and dislikes develop. Once the crib has been banished to the attic, or back to the nursery for child number two, the bedroom comes into its own, as the preschool child emerges, assertive and irrepressibly inventive.

Whereas many children once lived close enough to open green spaces, where they could safely frolic in meadows and romp in woods, creating dens, treasure islands, and imaginary worlds, their lives are often shaped today by a need to be supervised for their own safety, and by the dominant presence of the television, video recorder, and computer. The end of the twentieth century has brought with it a yearning for a return to simple values and to childhoods filled with simple magic once again.

During the last few decades children have been encouraged to become instant adults, missing out on some of the joys of innocent play. You can recapture the fun of childhood by making their rooms stimulating and inviting – a good starting point for fun and learning, health and happiness.

A vibrant room packed with toys and activities is ideal for the preschool child. In this Owl and the Pussycat Bedroom (see page 52), even the playhouse is decorated in colors that go with the room.

ADAPTATIONS

Turning a nursery into a preschool bedroom may be simply a matter of changing a crib for a bed, buying a wardrobe, and acquiring a small desk and chair. However, it is rarely so straightforward. As your baby becomes a small person, you will probably find yourself redecorating or deciding how to make the most of the available space in the room. Yet if you have planned the nursery with all these adaptations at the back of your mind, the transition should be relatively easy and, above all, fun.

Preschool siblings often share the same room, either owing to lack of space in the home or out of preference. For this arrangement to work well, try to reflect both personalities in your scheme. If one is a bookworm and the other an actor, make sure there is provision for plenty of bookshelves and a dressing-up corner. Try to provide varied storage, and give some thought to the beds. Two single beds that can be adapted to form bunks later on could be a good temporary solution.

DECORATING

The ages of two to five are the years in which your furnishings will get some of the heaviest wear and tear in terms of spills and rough treatment, so it's best to think ahead and plan your use of fabrics and wallpapers accordingly. A good way of allowing for the odd replacement of wallpaper or mop-up operation is to choose a kind of wallcovering that divides the wall in some way. A wallpaper border at chair rail height, with washable latex paint below, and striped, polkadotted, or floral paper above will prove a versatile solution for the "messy" years.

On the windows, it is a good idea to have some form of blackout lining to prevent early morning awakenings in the summer months. A

The sky at night is depicted in naive form in this simple stenciled frieze, transforming a part of the room that is often left plain white. A colorwash-stripe wallpaper provides the stripes. The design will appeal to any age group.

combination of a roller or Roman shade, backed with blackout lining, along with a pair of simple, lightweight curtains, is a good solution. Team them with a simple valance, scalloped for a feminine feel or zigzagged for boys, and you will have a complete window treatment that is both visually appealing and practical.

Young children adore color, so window treatments offer a good chance of combining contrasting colors or fabrics. Team polkadots with stripes, flowers with plain fabrics, and bold checks with small checks.

Allow your children to decide on a theme themselves and help decide where the images should appear – if you want to limit their impact, suggest a duvet cover emblazoned with a favorite animal or character and then echo the colors elsewhere in the room.

BEDS AND BED LINEN

The bed is the one piece of equipment that merits special thought, as it will probably last your child into the teenage years. Now is the time to consider a bunk bed if you have other children or are thinking of expanding the family, although children should not sleep on a top bunk before they are six years old. A platform bed or loft bed with a desk and den space underneath may be the answer for a small room, or a bed with baskets underneath in a traditional interior. Make sure that the mattress is firm and of good quality and that the bed is the right size. Some antique beds are quite short and narrow so would not last very long for a tall child.

You can, to some extent, dictate the feel of a bedroom by your choice of bed linen. If you have bold colored walls emblazoned with strong, simple motifs, then chances are you will need an equally vibrant duvet cover or bedspread.

If you are unable to find a ready-made duvet cover to suit you, you could make your own. It's a simple operation to choose fabric that goes with your scheme, give it a turn-over in a contrasting color trimmed with buttons, ties, or bows, and make a pillowcase to match – as we did for our Owl and the Pussycat Bedroom.

Contrasting fabric was used to trim this duvet cover with a buttoned turn-over, while the pillowcase was given a similar treatment. Details like these look just as smart in a preschool child's bedroom as in an older child's or adult's room.

A PLAY PALACE

Children of preschool age are highly social, thriving on the company of their contemporaries and relishing the busy days, full of creative pursuits and a rich fantasy life. To provide the ideal environment for children to immerse themselves in another world, it is worth putting some effort into making their rooms as interesting and magnetic as possible.

Play is an important part of the learning process of young children. Dressing-up games involving real or make-believe characters, games featuring the buying and selling of myriad items in pretend stores, and games involving miniature worlds of play people, soft toys, pirates, or soldiers, all help develop the imagination and emotions of a young child.

Another opportunity for your child to learn is through play-acting with plenty of props and equipment. A dressing-up box (maybe the blanket box you had in the nursery) is a favorite possession of many children and is often fondly remembered in later life. In fact, dressing-up boxes are essential equipment for young children. Their urge to step out of themselves and become a fairy or pirate, a soldier or angel, is very strong. A block-printed, stenciled, hand-painted, or decoupage chest or box in the corner of a room can neatly contain all the paraphernalia and be a decorative contribution to the room in its own right. The box in our Owl and the Pussycat Bedroom was simply glazed and then potato-printed with stars to match the stenciled stars around the top of the wall.

Simple treasure in the form of highly decorative dressing-up clothes will be donned much more often if stored in a magical painted box. This one was decorated with stars in accordance with our Owl and the Pussycat star and moon theme.

DISPLAYING TOYS

At this age, pigeonhole shelves come into their own, either as parts of a freestanding unit or built into an alcove or across an entire wall of the room. Use them for displaying distinct types of toys such as spinning tops, wooden animals, toy musical instruments, miniature tea-sets, cars, or books. Fill old printers' trays with antique wooden building blocks, dolls' house accessories, Noah's ark animals, brooches, and badges. Change the displays every so often and hide some things away from time to time in a cupboard or wardrobe – rediscovering toys is exciting, especially on wet winter days.

Miniature worlds in the form of dolls' houses, play houses, forts, and farms are popular toys at this stage, particularly when they have been made by parents or relatives. Make sure there is enough floor or table space for your child to spread out all the small accessories, such as people, animals, kitchen equipment, furniture, and scraps of fabric. They are the vital props that will bring these tiny scenes to life.

CREATING MORE STORAGE

When a nursery becomes more of a bedroom, you will inevitably need to find extra storage space. If the bed you have chosen is freestanding, capitalize on the space underneath it by adding drawers, baskets, or crates on castors. Stacking boxes or baskets are space-saving containers for building blocks and other small items. They will fit happily underneath a bottom shelf or at the foot of a wardrobe. In an underused alcove, consider fitting a chrome clothes rail at a height where your children can reach their own clothes. It will encourage them to dress themselves and exercise choice in what they wish to wear. (Make sure you display only the clothing you would like them to wear, though!) You can cover the alcove with a simple fabric shade. Simply insert eyelets along the top edge of the shade, lace cord through the holes, and lash it to a shelf fitted into the alcove above the rail.

Freestanding toy cupboards – securely screwed to the wall if there is any chance they could be pulled over – are versatile pieces of furniture. They can be painted to echo your decorative theme, or left plain and embellished with panels of fabric or wooden fretwork.

To keep small toys away from babies in the house, consider mounting open-topped wooden boxes onto the wall and painting the fronts with blackboard paint so they double as wall-mounted easels and toy boxes.

FLOORS AND WALLS

If you had a painted floor in the nursery, then there is no need to change it for this stage of childhood. Youngsters in this phase do everything at speed, so nonslip and wipeable flooring is a distinct advantage now. Cork tiles provide a neutral-colored, practical surface, while carpet tiles are individually replaceable should spills and stains spoil it in places. If nursery motifs have become too babyish, try painting the floor a totally different color.

Walls can become decorative elements in their own right. Children are delighted by big images which tell a story. If you feel inclined, try painting a scene from your child's favorite classic fairy tale, or nursery rhyme, or involving a well-loved cartoon character. If you use muted colors, you can always paint over the wall when the mural has been outgrown.

Encourage your child's creative skills by pinning their best efforts on a bulletin board and framing any particular favorites. Or create a special area of the wall to use for their pictures (see page 110).

Devise a frieze made up of your child's own images. Use a specific scene that bears repetition around the room – such as a vase of flowers, a simple house complete with polkadotted curtains, or stick figures – then photocopy the image, enlarging it if necessary. Ask your child to color in each one, then mount them together on the wall at chair rail height, using white craft glue. These borders are infinitely replaceable and children will love being able to create their own friezes for their rooms. At this age, children start to take an interest in height charts. Mount one on the wall near a doorway.

THE PRESCHOOL BEDROOM:
FURNISHING SUGGESTIONS

Bed with underbed storage, or bunk or platform bed

Small table and two chairs for creative activities

Painting easel

Height chart

Bulletin board for photographs, paintings, and drawings

Additional storage shelves or bookcase

Dressing-up box

THE OWL AND THE PUSSYCAT BEDROOM

Our Owl and the Pussycat Bedroom (shown on pages 46–47) was designed around the needs and interests of children aged from two to five. Children in this age group adore having a galaxy of activities strewn around their rooms. Nooks and crannies offering inviting space for play-houses and boxes of dressing-up clothes; small chairs and a table for mock tea parties; baskets laden with books; vibrant colors and their own artwork adorning the walls all make the room as appealing as possible.

This particular scheme uses bold colors that are suitable for either a girl or boy. The Owl and Pussycat wallpaper border, the starting point, suggests a star-and-moon theme in a blue and yellow color scheme. Striped wallpaper is contrasted with bold checked fabric and chambray-blue woodwork. Elsewhere in the room a bold checked fabric is used for the curtains and fabric-covered wardrobe. The bed linen fabric is a simple, painterly floral with a small check design in it that matches the chambray blue and apple green of the big check. All these fabrics and wallpapers use designs a child will not outgrow. (See page 29 for how they can be adapted as the child gets older.)

CUT-OUT LAMPSHADE

Lampshades can be adapted to match the decorative theme of a child's room. Trace some simple shapes (here the motifs echo the moons and stars on the walls above the picture rail) around a simple, round shade using a pencil; then, with an X-acto knife, carefully cut out the shapes. Alternatively, glue on small decorative pieces such as tiny shells, pieces of knotted rope, or sequins and buttons.

FOUR-POSTER BED FRAME

Wooden four-poster beds such as that shown here are fun to make but should only be tackled by someone with experience of carpentry. They can range from four simple posts draped with fabric to elaborate shapes formed with a jigsaw. Another idea is to attach shallow plywood panels that echo the base of the bed frame then stick on wallpaper borders, cut-out shapes, or three-dimensional images such as fabric animal motifs or wooden building blocks. Alternatively, paint shapes on by hand, or stencil or sponge pretty patterns for a slightly different effect.

This bed frame simply fits over an existing divan bed. The easiest way to construct it is by building it in situ. Use 2 x 2in (5 x 5cm) posts at the corners; ours are 79in (2m) high, but the exact height will depend on the height of your ceiling. Be sure to allow adequate clearance above the bed. When planning the horizontal dimensions of the framework, allow a little room between the frame and the mattress for bedding.

The posts are joined with eight 12in (30cm) deep lengths of ½in (1.25cm) thick fiberboard; use four at the bottom (at divan height) and four at the top as a cornice.

Cut star shapes out of the cornice strips at regular intervals using a drill and a jigsaw, then attach all eight lengths of fiberboard with countersunk screws. Paint the whole framework, and decorate the base with a wallpaper border.

PLAYHOUSE

This easy-to-construct playhouse has three hinged walls and a removable roof. It could be further simplified by making it in hardboard and dispensing with the roof. If it can be put in a corner, it can have just two walls, making it more portable. Children will love going in and out the doorway, so add to their fun with a mailbox and a bicycle bell for a doorbell.

MEASURING

Decide how big a playhouse you would like and cut out three pieces of fiberboard accordingly. (You do not need a fourth piece because the open side of the house will be against a wall.) If you wish the walls to fold flat for storage, the two side walls will have to be no more than half the width of the middle wall.

1 Taking the piece of fiberboard for the front of the house first, cut out the main window with a jigsaw. Use water-based paint to transform it into a house or a shop. Remember to paint both sides, as one will be inside the house. Next, cut four 2in (5cm) strips of fiberboard to fit around the window. Paint these a different color from the walls if you wish. Screw in place. Small pieces can be glued instead.

2 Cut out a window and door opening and repeat the process for the door wall, but use a 3in (7.5cm) strip of fiberboard for the bottom horizontal piece of the door frame. Paint. Repeat again for the third wall.

3 The simplest method of joining the three panels together is to affix two long metal hinges to the inside edges where each panel joins the next, so the walls can be folded flat. Covering the hinged edge with strong, thick tape will add strength and prevent children from scratching themselves, but will

prevent it from folding up. Similarly, vertical supports can be added on the inside at the corners for extra strength, but these too will prevent the playhouse from folding flat.

4 For the door, cut a piece of fiberboard to fit the opening. Cut a hole in it for the mailbox, then cut a piece of fiberboard for the flap. Attach this over the opening with hinges, covering the hinged edge with the tape.

5 Finally, attach the door to the door frame with hinges, and paint the whole surface.

6 To make the serving hatch shelf, cut a piece of fiberboard 4in (10cm) wide, and as long as you want the shelf to be. Paint it, then leave to dry. Attach it to the window frame with strong, thick tape. Allow the shelf to fold down when not in use. To hold it up when it is being used, fix hooks to the upper surface of the shelf and attach the

YOU WILL NEED

½IN (1.25CM) THICK FIBERBOARD,
PLYWOOD, OR HARDBOARD
METAL HINGES
STRONG, THICK TAPE
WOODEN DOWEL
JIGSAW
METAL CHAIN, HOOKS, AND SCREW EYES
NAILS AND SCREWS
WOODEN DOOR KNOB
WOOD GLUE
WATER-BASED PAINTS
BICYCLE BELL

metal chains to the inside edge of the window frame.

7 Make and attach the serving hatch door in the same way but attach the hooks to its bottom outside edge and the screw eyes to the roof.

8 Made from four pieces of fiberboard, the roof is hinged down the middle and on both sloping edges of each end. For strength you ccould cover the hinged edges with the black tape. Dowels can also be used to give the roof additional rigidity. Drill two holes (shaped like elongated circles to allow for the slope) on the front and two more, in line with the first two, on the back, then insert the dowels. Finally, paint the whole surface.

WARDROBE

Fabric-covered wardrobes like this delightful checked one are wonderfully versatile storage solutions for children's rooms. Choose a wooden shelf unit, or shelves plus a hanging rail, to cover with the fabric. As your child grows, you can either remove the fabric to reveal a simple set of storage shelves or change the fabric cover to suit the child's new tastes.

YOU WILL NEED

WOOD FRAME
FABRIC
MATCHING SEWING THREAD

MEASURING

This wardrobe is 73in (185cm) high, 47in (120cm) wide, and 36in (91cm) deep, but you can adjust the measurements as much as you wish.

For the back, cut a panel of fabric the width of the back plus 1½in (4cm), by the height of the back plus 2½in (6.5cm). For the sides, cut two panels each the width of the side plus 1½in (4cm), by the height of the side plus 2½in (6.5cm). For the front, cut two panels each half the width of the front plus 2¼in (6cm), by the height of the front plus 2½in (6.5cm). Remember when cutting the panels to insure the pattern matches all the way around.

A 1½in (4cm) hem is included in the above measurements, but if you prefer a deeper one – in the picture the hem is 5in (13cm) or so – add extra to each panel. If you are using very wide fabric or making a cover for a small wardrobe, you may be able to cut the front and side panels as one piece, or possibly even use just two panels, which meet at center back.

For the top, cut a panel the width of the frame plus 1½in (4cm), by the depth of the frame plus 1½in (4cm).

For the zigzag edge, cut 9in (23cm) wide strips on the bias. Join to form two strips as long as the width of the frame plus twice the depth of the frame plus 6in (15cm), being careful to match the pattern.

For the four ties, cut four 16 x 2in (40.5 x 5cm) strips on the straight grain.

1 With right sides together and raw edges even, stitch each front panel to a side panel, taking a ¾in (2cm) seam and matching the pattern at the seamline. Stitch the side panels to the back panel in the same way.

2 Turn under ½in (1.25cm) and then 1½in (4cm) on the center front edge and on the lower edge all around. Press and stitch.

3 To make the ties, fold the long raw edges of each strip to meet in the center, then fold in half lengthwise. Press and stitch, turning under the raw edges at each end. Hand sew the ties to the wrong side on both front opening edges, positioning one pair about a quarter of the way down and the other pair about halfway down.

4 For the zigzag edging, place the fabric strips with right sides together and raw edges even. Make a zigzag template with the triangles each 5in (12.5cm) high. Place it 3in (7.5cm) from the fold and ½in (1.25cm) from each end; draw around the template. Stitch along the marked lines. Trim the fabric ¼in (6mm) from the stitching, cutting off the outer corners and clipping into the inner corners within the seam allowance. Turn right side out and press. Turn in the raw edges at the ends, press and slipstitch.

5 On the right side, pin and baste the zigzag piece around the top, with the raw edges even.

6 Turn under and press ¾in (2cm) on all four edges of the top panel. With right sides together, pin, baste and stitch the joined front, side, and back panels (and zigzag edging) to the top panel, matching the seams to the corners and stitching one side at a time so you can stop at the seamline in each corner. Clip into the corners within the seam allowance. Remove any remaining basting that is visible, and then press.

THE AMAZON BEDROOM

You can almost hear the Amazonian waterfalls and far-off screeching parakeets in this jungle-inspired room. Using the multicolored wallpaper border as a starting point, we drew on the wild-life motifs to create a tropical den. The bed, with its camouflage canopy, is the tent from which explorers venture forth after a cozy night's sleep. The hammock harbors teddies and dolls, where they can keep dry, and the rug, complete with menacing crocodile, is the place where you play at your peril. Fabrics are kept plain and simple as befits a rugged tropical outpost, but colors are vivid jungle tones of blue-green, red, and orange.

At this age, children will love to join in decision-making and helping with simple tasks. Many of the smaller projects involve cutting out and gluing, which are ideal for small children. They will delight in attaching their finished creations to the walls and other surfaces.

Dripping with jungle imagery, our Amazon Bedroom is more an adventure playground than a bedroom. Translucent tropical-green walls seem to extend all over the room, with similar shades on toy boxes and bed curtains, while animals are everywhere, apparently leaping out from the wallpaper border to adorn rugs, curtains, and the bed. Tie-top curtains with boldly colored borders and appliquéd parkeets serve the dual purpose of blocking out the light and adding to the jungle scene.

GIRAFFE EASEL

Customize a painting easel to match the mood of the day or the room theme. Children will love to make their own decisions about this. Encourage them to paint whole pictures or patterns.

JUNGLE BOX

Painted in two shades of rain forest green, this chest can be used for jungle clothes and pith helmet – or simply as a place to keep clutter. Decorate it with animal stickers or cut-out images from the wallpaper border to echo the other animals in the room. You could also photocopy the images so your child can color them in. Alternatively, paint on palm trees and banana leaves or bamboo and bulrushes. After painting the box and gluing the images on, apply several coats of varnish, allowing it to dry between coats.

CHANGING JUNGLE SCENE

To complete the jungle fever theme, create a movable felt picture, in which children can move the constituent parts around to create their own jungle scenes. Cover a standard cork bulletin board with deep green felt, attaching the felt at the back with a staple gun or fabric glue. Next, attach vertical strips of self-adhesive Velcro®. These represent the trunks of palm trees. Cut out palm fronds and jungle animals from felt, and affix Velcro® on the back of each. Children can then arrange and rearrange the animals against the background of palm trees.

GLAZED WALLS

The subtle forest green walls of our Amazon Bedroom are created by applying a pale yellow basecoat to the wall. When it is dry, a coat of blue-green water-based paint, diluted to a thin wash, is lightly applied on top to create a vivid but translucent texture, evoking a tropical rain forest. You can also buy wallpapers that imitate this paint effect.

BUNK BED COVER

This tent-like bunk bed cover is formed from three canvas panels, attached to the bed frame with Velcro®. It transforms the bed into a jungle playhouse for intrepid explorers and even incorporates a roll-up window. The tropical vegetation has been applied with acrylic paint, but fabric paint is equally effective and is washable. Or decorate the tent using appliquéd, stenciled, or sponged designs.

MEASURING

Measure the bunk bed to establish the size of the panels, and add ¼ in (4.5cm) all around for hems.

1 Cut out three canvas panels. If your fabric isn't wide enough, join widths using flat felt seams. Hem all four edges of each panel by pressing under ¼in (5mm) and then 1½in (4cm); machine stitch, mitering the corners (see page 41, step 10).

2 On one side panel, create a window by cutting out a rectangle about the size of this book. Make a 2in (5cm) snip diagonally into each corner. Turn under the raw edges to make a double hem on each edge; stitch.

3 From the remaining fabric, cut out the flap so that it is 5in (13cm) wider than the window opening and 5½in (14.5cm) deeper. Stitch a double ½in (1.25cm) hem on the side and bottom edges. For the two straps, cut two strips of fabric, each measuring 3½in x 12in (9 x 30.5cm). Fold each in half, right sides together, and stitch down the side and across one end, taking a

¼in (5mm) seam. Turn the straps right side out.

4 To attach the window flap to the panel, position it above the window opening, right sides together, with the raw edge of the flap ½in (1.25cm) above the top of the window. Insert the two straps between the flap and the panel, with the raw edges even with those of the flap. Stitch across the flap, taking a 1½in (4cm) seam. Turn

down the flap so it covers the window opening, with the straps hanging down on top. Attach snaps to the ends, with the other halves on the panel just above the window opening. Use the straps to hold the flap when rolled up.

5 On the other side panel, attach an eyelet at the bottom (at the edge that will be in the center). Thread a length of cord through it, and use it to tie the panel back onto the bed frame. You could also attach one to the side panel with the window if you want to.

6 Machine stitch the sew-on side of a strip of Velcro® to the top edge of each panel and stick the self-adhesive side to the bed frame.

7 Decorate the panels by whichever method you choose. If you use fabric paints, fix them following the manufacturer's directions so the panels will be hand-washable.

TIE-TOP JUNGLE CURTAINS

These cheery jungle curtains, replete with vividly colored parakeets, will enliven any window view. Unlined for simplicity, they are finished off with bound edges and ties, and can match or contrast with your chosen motifs for the bunk bed cover. Either fabric or felt can be used for making the bird shapes but, if you use felt, you'll have to dry-clean the curtains rather than wash them.

YOU WILL NEED

MAIN CURTAIN FABRIC
CONTRASTING FABRIC
MATCHING SEWING THREAD
FELT OR FABRIC FOR APPLIQUÉ SHAPES
FUSIBLE WEB
STRANDED EMBROIDERY FLOSS

MEASURING

For the curtain fabric, you will need a little less than 1½ times the width of the pole, since too much fullness would obscure the appliquéd birds. To calculate the length, measure from the pole to wherever you want the curtains to end, and add 6in (15cm).

1 Cut out the curtains from the main fabric, and join widths if necessary. From the contrasting fabric, cut 4in (10cm) wide strips on the straight grain. Join the ends until you have enough to bind all around the edges of the curtains. Fold the binding in half lengthwise, wrong sides together, and press. Now fold the raw edges in almost to the center, and press.

2 Encase the raw edges of the curtain sides and bottom in the folded binding. Pin in place and topstitch. Miter the corners at the bottom end by folding the binding diagonally. Finally, bind the top edge in the same way, turning in the raw ends at each side rather than mitering the corners.

3 The curtain ties are made from strips of a different color but the same type of fabric. Cut out enough 18 x 2in (45 x 5cm) strips for your curtain width, allowing for them to be spaced about 8in (20.5cm) apart. Turn under ¼in (6mm) on each long side and press. Fold the strips in half lengthwise, wrong sides together, then press again. Stitch the folded sides together. Sew the strips securely to the back of the curtain, at the top.

4 Use the templates at the back of the book to cut out the parakeet shapes from fusible web. Iron the shapes onto pieces of felt, following the manufacturer's directions, then cut out the shapes in felt. Peel off the backing paper and iron the felt shapes to the right side of the curtain. Embroider around the outer edges using a large slipstitch or a large cross-stitch and several strands of embroidery floss.

TEDDIES' HAMMOCK

This cotton hammock provides a restful, not to mention tidy, retreat for the dolls and soft toys. If you want it to hold a very large collection of soft toys, hang it in a corner, perhaps attached to the wall and a bed, as here, or to a peg rail fixed onto adjacent walls. Be sure to hang it where a child cannot try to climb into it.

YOU WILL NEED

THICK CANVAS OR
UPHOLSTERY-WEIGHT FABRIC
MATCHING SEWING THREAD
12 LARGE EYELETS AND EYELET TOOL
2 LARGE CURTAIN RINGS
WHITE CORD

1 Cut a 36 x 48in (90 x 120cm) piece of fabric. Fold in half crosswise with right sides together. Stitch a ½in (1.25cm) seam down the side, leaving an opening for turning right side out.

2 Refold so that the seam runs down the middle. Stitch across both ends taking a ½in (1.25cm) seam. Trim seams and clip corners. Turn right side out, slipstitch the opening, and press.

3 Using the eyelet tool, attach eyelets at 2in (5cm) intervals at both ends.

4 At each end, lace a length of cord back and forth through the eyelets and the curtain ring.

5 Hang the finished hammock on two fixed hooks or on one hook and the bed frame.

APPLIQUÉD SWAMP RUG

This decorated rug doubles as a playmat, instantly becoming a treacherous swamp whenever a child wishes. Use a bright, nubbly cotton rug as your backdrop and create a scene or still life on a water theme. If crocodiles are too frightening, then apply some waterlilies and a few leaping frogs, or a fishing fleet and a shoal of mackerel. A green rug could form a meadow for dragonflies, small birds, and ripening wheat, or a bold swath of sunflowers.

1 Using the templates at the back of the book, cut out the shapes, adding a ¼in (6mm) seam allowance all around to the fabric shapes. (Felt shapes do not need a seam allowance.) Cut the stepping stones from the beige linen or jute. Cut the main part of the crocodile from the lighter green fabric. Cut the crocodile's scaly back from the darker green fabric as follows: Using the wide template, cut four pieces of which two are in reverse; using the short, narrow template, cut one piece; using the long, narrow template, cut two pieces of which one is in reverse. Cut the crocodile's features and the waterlilies from felt.

2 Turn under ¼in (6mm) all around the edges of the stepping stones and zigzag stitch. Stitch the flower centers to the flowers. Turn under a narrow hem all around the edges of the crocodile's body and head; stitch.

3 Stitch a long, narrow dart down the center of the crocodile's head, on the right side. Stitch the crocodile's eyes to his head, gluing on the black felt pieces. For his nostrils, cut two

crescent shapes from the green felt nose, and back the holes with black felt; stitch around the edge of each nostril then stitch the nose to the head.

4 Join the segments of the crocodile, with right sides together, taking ¼in (6mm) seams.

5 For the wide part of the scaly back, pin one of the wide shapes to its mirror image, right sides together, and stitch along the straight edge taking a ¼in (6mm) seam. Repeat for the other two identical shapes. Now lay these two pieces with right sides together, and stitch all around the edges, taking a ¼in (6mm) seam and leaving an opening. Turn right side out, press and slipstitch the opening.

6 For the piece that goes on top, turn under ¼in (6mm) all around the short, narrow back piece and press. Center it on top of the wide back piece and stitch around the edge of the top piece. Now hand sew the whole piece to the crocodile's body.

7 Pin the two long, narrow back pieces with right sides together. Stitch all around the edge, taking a ¼in (6mm) seam and leaving an opening in the straight side for turning. Turn right side out, press, and stitch to the crocodile's tail along the straight edge.

8 Position the crocodile diagonally across the rug, and the stepping stones so they meander across the other diagonal. Scatter the waterlilies over the remaining surface. Hand sew all the pieces in place around the edges.

CHAPTER FIVE

The Grade School Years

Once children start school, their lives and yours change dramatically. Their independence, already established with small friends arriving for tea and play, is further extended, with after-school activities and weekend visits further afield. This is the age when most boys and girls, who may have previously played happily together for hours on end, become polarized for a while – the boys not wishing to be associated with girls and their dolls, the girls disliking too much rough and tumble in the playground.

School also means a compulsion to be like everyone else, the necessity for possessing the latest toy craze, and a need to collect all sorts of ephemera and natural booty, from garish stickers to flotsam and jetsam from the beach. All these extra possessions will need extra storage space, both small-scale and large-scale. Children of this age will certainly have an opinion about their rooms, with very specific color preferences. Where possible, encourage them to partake in any redecoration or space-planning jobs. They may particularly enjoy applying motifs to walls, floor, and fixtures or painting shapes onto muslin for making up into small curtains.

A life on the ocean waves seems perfectly possible in this Sailor's Bedroom (see page 74). Armed with a huge boat bed that looks almost seaworthy, real sails, and lengths of bunting, adventurous children can immerse themselves in all sorts of imaginary nautical adventures. Jaunty stripes in the classic color combination of red, white, and blue adorn duffel bags, simple window shades, bunting, and pillows, while boat motifs appear on the duvet fabric and are appliquéd to crisp white pillowcases.

ROOM TO GROW

Older grade-school children tend to spend most of their time in their rooms, playing with friends, or at the kitchen table, seeking help with difficult homework. They are constantly on the go, creating wear, tear, and torture on all sorts of indoor surfaces from floors and walls to fabric and furniture, so make sure that any new furniture you acquire at this stage will withstand the rigorous treatment of swinging, climbing, and performing youngsters.

Children of this age group appreciate as much space as possible to spread out train sets, farmyards, miniature car sets, and complicated board games. Since accidental spills and messy play lessen to some extent at this stage, you could quite happily lay durable carpeting. Or, if you prefer wooden floorboards, you could think about investing in a rug, which will last until your child leaves home and could then be pressed into service elsewhere.

An area of the room devoted to study is essential now. It should comprise a desk, a serviceable lamp, and a sturdy chair, together with shelving for books, a wastebasket, and, ideally, an additional work/play surface. This comes in handy for homework that needs extra space and also as a place to keep small pets such as guinea pigs, hamsters, tadpoles, or goldfish, not to mention miniature gardens and collections of shells, stones, twigs, and leaves. Children of this age seem to accumulate treasures from a variety of sources, including school, friends, and the great outdoors.

Don't discard any miniature tables and chairs your preschool child may have used. They will still be very useful for playing card and board games and for practicing reading and writing.

Try to incorporate a small, freestanding mirror and brush and comb to encourage youngsters to smarten themselves up before leaving for school. Girls in particular enjoy having some kind of dressing table in which they can store their jewelry and knick-knacks. The easiest way to create one would be to cover a circular table in the fabric of her choice. The top of a chest of drawers gives ample opportunity for a miniature dressing table, complete with small wicker baskets containing scarves and hats. Boys may be more content with a basketful of sports equipment, squirt guns, and trading cards.

DECORATING

At this age, children particularly like themed rooms. Our Sailor's Bedroom, shown on pages 68–69, is a young boy's dream. Inspired by the fabric used for the duvet, which has boats, planes, and cars on it, it has been designed around a specially built bed. Everything else in the room could easily be adapted once the child has outgrown this particular passion. But, in the meantime, where better to fend off marauding pirates than from the comfort and safety of your own bed, complete with "secret" storage compartments in the stern for hidden treasure. At the other end of the room, a real dinghy – preferably a small one – piled with pillows could provide a reading area, as well as a wonderful setting for a game.

Other popular themes include knights and heraldic symbols, toy soldiers, circuses, and sports motifs. A border of cut-out life-sized soccerballs could divide a wall graphically, as would a series of heraldic shields or banners, colored in different tones and styles. Appliqué similar shapes onto plain fabric or use a particular themed border as the starting point for a scheme.

For girls, try simple flower shapes, or floral fabrics, simple checks and stripes, or a polka-dotted pattern with differing sizes of dots, on bed linen, window treatments, and ruffles around a tabletop. Team with a valance embellished with bows, or make a simple tie shade with fabric rosettes ranged across it at regular intervals. To provide some contrast with accessories, cover boxes, line baskets, or make drawstring bags in contrasting fabrics.

Box-seat cushions, bolsters, and throws are another useful way of incorporating fabric in a room, providing a good counterpoint to the bed linen and curtains.

The fabrics chosen for both our Little Princess's Bedroom (see page 83) and the Sailor's Bedroom are not particularly childish in style. However, they have been used in an imaginative way: four-poster-style bed hangings, or strings of flags flying above a bed, create the feeling that the bed is sailing on the high seas or set in a

Painted furniture is a successful way of enhancing the decoration in a room. Use matching or contrasting colors, add cut-out shapes or painted imagery – such as the painted portholes of this boat bed in our Sailor's Bedroom (page 74) – and protect the finished product with a coat of water-based varnish.

fairy-tale castle. At this stage of childhood, using adult fabrics can work very well. Fresh-looking checks, simple stripes, and subtly patterned damask all work for both sexes and are durable as well as pleasing. They can be used in any number of ways, such as plain window shades, window-seat covers, pleated bed skirts, simple hangings that curtain off a bed, or gently gathered curtains combined with a crenellated or scalloped cornice.

For a shade for open shelves, or to make a bedcover, floorcloth, wall hanging, or door curtain, buy plain canvas and paint colorful patterns or motifs that have been chosen by your child onto it. (The waves on page 78 are very simple to achieve.)

Another good way to unify a scheme is to use fabric or wallpaper to cover rough-edged tea chests for toy storage. Or paint metal trunks and decorate them with decoupaged shapes or motifs to blend in with the theme – whether pirates, cartoon characters, or bunches of flowers.

If your child has definitely outgrown the design on their bed linen, make a new duvet cover and pillow sham, or appliqué motifs onto plain muslin using blanket stitch.

At this age, children are capable of helping you with painting or decorating jobs. Enlist their help in sanding and painting furniture, choosing fabric, and deciding on motifs. They will enjoy looking in magazines and catalogs for inspiration. Let them tell you what they like before you unconsciously impose your preferences on them. Give them the confidence to express their likes and dislikes, even if their taste is not quite the same as yours – you can always accommodate their choices on smaller details such as cupboard door panels, headboards, or wall friezes.

STORAGE

You will still need to store some preschool toys in this older child's room, so they can be rediscovered from time to time. Older children take great nostalgic comfort from their early toys and enjoy renewed acquaintance with their younger years every so often.

Additional storage space is likely to be needed for new possessions such as games, chemistry sets, musical instruments, binoculars, and flower presses. Either add on extra shelves to an existing system or think about a freestanding cupboard or chest of drawers for tidying away board games and sports equipment. A fabric-covered wardrobe (page 56) is as valuable now as in a younger child's room.

Extra storage can always be created in a modular bed system or by devoting one wall or alcove to fitted pigeonholes. Vary their sizes so you can fit in anything from encyclopedias to baseball mitts, rag dolls to footballs.

A bedside table is useful at this age, for an alarm clock, a light, some reading matter, and a drink. It also encourages a child to develop some independence in the mornings and evenings.

Fabric wall pockets are useful for tidying away slippers and sneakers, as well as dressing-up scarves, hats, and shoes.

If you decide to buy a bed that is a modular unit of some kind, think about installing a shelving system within a canopied bed (see page 90) or underneath the mattress. Or, if space permits, place the bed away from one wall and put a chest of drawers up against it, to double as a headboard and additional storage space.

HOMEWORK CORNER

Children will spend increasing amounts of time at their desks. Make sure that the chair supports the child's back well and is the right size for the type of desk. Position a gooseneck lamp or other desk lamp on or near the desk. If there are younger children in the house, check that no electrical cords are exposed.

Fix a bulletin board above or to the side of the desk and insure that a bookcase or wall-mounted shelves are nearby for storing reference books. If space is limited, fit castor wheels to a wooden box and tie a rope handle to it. This will become a mobile storage unit for paints or craft activities that need to be out of reach of younger hands, and can double as a small table for drinks and snacks. Combine it with a couple of bean bags so it can serve as a social area when your child's friends come to play.

Use the walls for educational posters such as maps, nature charts, or word and number cards. Get your child to help in compiling a photo-collage of all his or her relatives. Include as many generations as you can find and tell them snippets of family history while you make it.

As this is the age when children formally learn to read and write, make sure there is plenty of book storage and enough pens and pencils in appealing pots, as well as a prominently displayed clock, for learning to tell the time.

Some child-height storage – either deep, open shelves or a chest with shallow drawers – would be useful for storing precious paintings, work-books, and other "projects," such as scrapbooks, photograph albums, and family trees.

THE GRADE SCHOOL CHILD'S BEDROOM:
FURNISHING SUGGESTIONS

Bed with good mattress

Bedside table and lamp

Homework desk, task light, and chair

Dressing table and/or mirror

Additional work/play surface

Hanging storage and drawers or shelves for clothes

Storage for games, sports equipment, and craft materials

In our specially created Sailor's Bedroom an understated homework corner blends easily with the shipshape decor. A simple lamp, a substantial desk, and a map of the world all help to concentrate the young mind, while the daylight from the roof window provides good light for working and reading during the daytime.

BEDS AND BEDDING

Bunk beds come into their own with this age group. It is now safe for older children to clamber up to a top bunk to sleep, while the younger members of the age group should not fear storytime up there before settling down to slumber in the bottom bunk.

Bunks are especially useful if two children are sharing a room or as a permanent guest bed in an only child's room, for cousins and friends to use when they spend the night. Alternatively, visiting children can sleep on a temporary foam mattress and sleeping bag and the mattress can either be stored upright in a closet or be tucked under a bed elsewhere in the house.

THE SAILOR'S BEDROOM

This gloriously nautical room (shown on pages 68–69) is packed with decorating ideas on a sailing theme – everything that an enthusiastic pirate or sailor might need for a swashbuckling adventure on the high seas. Stripes are an enduring design, suitable for boys and girls, and ageless in their application. Use candlewick string for accessories and let your imagination inspire you to paint seashore scenes, create decoupage pictures of shells and treasure maps, sew laundry kit bags, hang sails or flags from the bedposts, or make a bed skirt with portholes. Encourage children to come up with their own nautical ideas.

A simple boat made from scraps of wood or even a cardboard box, combined with jute or canvas remnants, will delight youngsters. Paint the wood in bright nautical colors and ask your child to come up with a name or number to paint on the hull. Children are always inspired by boats, the sea, and the seashore so there will be no shortage of ideas from them.

BOAT BED

Hidden inside this colorful boat, which requires carpentry skills to construct, is a conventional bed frame made from 2 x 2in (5 x 5cm) horizontal wood supports, on which rest wooden slats that go underneath the mattress.

The outer structure is made from thin sheets of fiberboard cut to shape and screwed to 3 x 2in (7.5 x 5cm) lengths of wood. For the sloping edges, the wood was cut at graduating angles; because fiberboard is quite a pliable material, it curves gently around the wood to form the boat shape. It is easiest to build the sections separately then screw them together in situ. The shelf section is slipped over the back end, and screwed in place. Fitting castors to the bottom will allow it to be moved.

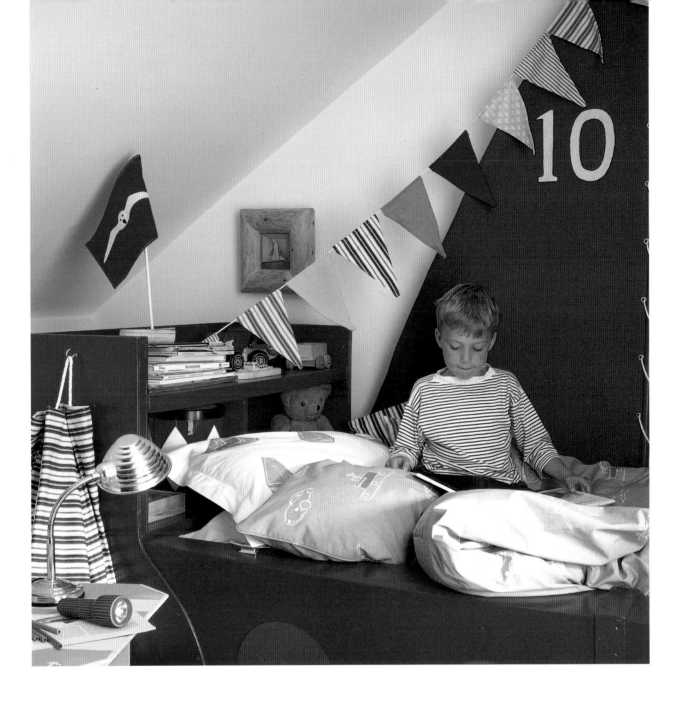

To make each sail, cut a right-angled triangle from canvas, and hem all three sides. Insert eyelets at about 5in (12.5cm) intervals down the vertical edge of the mainsail, and lash to the mast with white cord. In the other sail insert eyelets at the corners; using white cord, tie the sail to the top of the mast and to the bottom of the bed. Cut a number (or name) from fusible interfacing, and iron onto the sail.

For the bunting, cut diamond shapes from a variety of striped and plain fabrics. Turn under and press a narrow seam allowance to the wrong side on the raw edges. Fold in half and stitch the triangles down the remaining two edges, wrong sides together, stitching close to the edge, and starting/stopping about ⅜in (1cm) from the top. Thread the bunting onto cord and tie the cord to the top of the mast and the bed.

STRIPY QUILT

Red and blue striped fabrics look great together in a patchwork quilt. Complete with rope hand-holds, the quilt is just what budding sailors need to keep them warm on voyages. Choose a selection of different striped fabrics in nautical reds and blues, then follow the instructions for the Patchwork Crib Quilt on page 40, increasing the size and omitting the small-check and plain borders. When arranging the patchwork pieces, combine squares, rectangles, and triangles, and also make some squares with mitered borders (see page 41, step 3). Use different sizes so the effect will be similar to crazy patchwork. When wrapping the backing fabric over the batting to form an outer border, catch a length of cord into the seam at regular intervals.

SEAWORTHY COZY CORNER

Whatever your chosen decorative theme, a "real-life" prop or piece of scenery will add a touch of humor and adventure to the scheme. Here, a rowboat provides a quiet reading area in a busy boy's bedroom. The idea of climbing aboard a dinghy armed with favorite books and teddies, a cozy quilt, and no doubt a few snacks and a flashlight at night, will be irresistible to any imaginative seven-year-old. Alternatively, you could fence off a corner with twine and brass poles, and furnish it with squashy bean bag chairs covered in ticking or plain muslin.

CUSTOMIZED FLAGS

Ship to shore, the flags shown opposite and on page 75 are versatile adornments for headboards or wall displays, and will add the finishing touch to a run of bunting or a painting easel. Use them to create a wall display by placing one over another to form a cross shape or as a means of demarcating areas within a room. They could also be used to finish off a wigwam (see page 112) or puppet theater (see page 116).

To make each flag, cut two rectangles from a plain-colored fabric. Iron on stiff interfacing to the wrong side of one piece. On both pieces press under the edges by ¼in (6mm) all around. Glue a thick wooden skewer or plastic pole to the interfaced piece, then lay the other piece over it, wrong sides together. Topstitch all around the edges using white thread.

Enlarge a motif from the back of the book, or draw a design on tracing paper. We have used a skull-and-crossbones and a seagull, but other possibilities are a reef knot, an anchor, or the child's initials or name. Transfer the design to white felt (and black felt for the seagull's eyes and beak), cut out, and glue to the flag.

STOWAWAY STORAGE

Old luggage trunks are versatile and sturdy receptacles for toy debris. No matter how tidy children may be, they accumulate huge quantities of bits and pieces, from discarded teddy bears to hundreds of miniature toys. Stow them all away in spacious trunks decorated with nautical motifs and you won't have to worry about containing the clutter for a while.

Either cover the trunks with nautical wallpaper or else paste ocean-going emblems onto the surface; anything from cut-up old-style maps to pirate motifs or sailing symbols is

perfect. For extra authenticity, replace any broken handles or straps with rope. (If a trunk looks too new, just stain it with tea to "age" it.) And if the end result looks too good for old toys, use the trunk as a blanket box instead.

Wooden boxes or orange crates are another good form of roomy storage if sanded down thoroughly. (Watch out too for nails and sharp corners.) Here, we covered wooden boxes with wallpaper, painting the rims and edging them with thick sea-blue paper. They can be lined with plain paper or fabric.

WAVY SHADES

These hand-painted shades hide away toy clutter in the roof eaves. Make the shades from a single thickness of cream-colored canvas, hemming the edges and attaching to the wall with sew-and-stick Velcro®. Insert eyelets at the bottom

corners and also halfway up, to enable you to fold up the shade so that the waves are still visible. To paint on the waves, use a deep blue fabric paint, having first lightly marked out the shapes with a pencil.

PAINTED MURAL

For the sea in this simple mural, a water-based paint was diluted with water to create the washed out effect. Mark out your drawing freehand or, if the imagery is complicated, trace it, transfer the tracing to the wall, and then paint it in. To preserve the finished mural, apply an even coat of acrylic varnish. Children will love to help with a project like this, so choose at least one image they can paint themselves.

NAUTICAL SHADE

A jaunty solution for skylights or roof windows, this stripy shade keeps out the light yet looks crisp and stylish when clipped back. Attached with Velcro® to the wall itself, the shade also helps to disguise the window recess.

MEASURING

Decide how much of the wall around the window you want the shade to cover. You'll need to cut a piece of fabric twice the length of this area plus 2½in (6.5cm), and the width of the area plus 1in (2.5cm). The dowel will need to be 4in (10cm) shorter than the width of the fabric.

YOU WILL NEED

MAIN FABRIC
MATCHING SEWING THREAD
½IN (1.25CM) DIAMETER DOWEL
SEW-AND-STICK VELCRO®
LARGE EYELETS AND EYELET TOOL
4 AWNING CLEATS

1 Fold the piece of fabric in half crosswise, with right sides together, and stitch a ½in (1.25cm) seam down each long side. Turn the fabric right side out and press.

2 Place the dowel inside the shade, along the fold at the bottom, and stitch alongside it to form a casing around the dowel.

3 Apply an eyelet at each bottom corner of the shade, on either side of the length of dowelling.

4 At the top, press under ½in (1.25cm) and then 1½in (4cm). Stitch the sew-on side of the Velcro® to this top edge. Stick the self-adhesive side of the Velcro® to the wall above the window and attach the shade to this.

5 Screw two cleats to the wall at the bottom and another two cleats three-quarters of the way up on either side. Secure one corner of the shade by slotting the eyelet onto the cleat at the bottom, then fold back the opposite corner and hold it in place on the higher cleat on that side.

DUFFEL BAGS

No self-respecting sailor would be without his duffel bag. These durable ticking bags are endlessly useful for laundry, shoes, or dressing-up clothes, and can also double as overnight bags.

To make a duffel bag, you'll need to cut a circular base, a narrow rectangle, and a wider rectangle of fabric. Each rectangle should be as long as the circumference of the circle plus seam allowances. Their width together should add up to the desired height of the bag plus seam allowances. Cut one rectangle on the lengthwise grain and the other on the crosswise grain. Iron stiff fusible interfacing to the narrow rectangle. Join the rectangles along one long edge, and then join the ends of the piece to form a ring. Hem the top edge, and join the lower edge to the base. Add eyelets around the top edge, then lace the cord through them.

WALL POCKETS

This wall catchall is the perfect solution for tidying away shoes, craft aprons, and all the other small, loose paraphernalia children collect effortlessly and in great quantities. Here we have used cream-colored canvas, but you could use any robust upholstery fabric, patterned or plain, to suit the room. Our pockets are designed with a nautical theme in mind, but you could choose letters, numbers, or simple flower or animal shapes as decoration instead.

The instructions here are for a lined and interfaced catchall, which will be sturdy and hard-wearing, but if you use heavy canvas, you will probably not need to line or interface it; you can just hem the edges instead.

Make your pocket system to a size that is appropriate for your wall, and decide what you are going to store in it so that the pockets can be of varying sizes to contain the clutter. Make some pockets work as simple "slots" for thin books, and others with deep pleats to allow chunky shoes or other thick items to fit within easily. We have used small pockets in the top row, medium-sized ones in the middle row, and large ones in the bottom row, with pleats in proportion to the size of the pocket.

YOU WILL NEED

MAIN FABRIC
FABRICS FOR POCKETS AND FOR POCKET DECORATION
MATCHING SEWING THREAD
HEAVYWEIGHT FUSIBLE INTERFACING
STRONG DOWEL
2 HOOKS

MEASURING

Decide on the size of your finished hanging and draw it out on graph paper. Next, decide on the size and style of the pockets and draw outlines of them onto the plan, calculating how many you need and their exact dimensions. Be sure to allow 2in (5cm) or so above each row of pockets, and a further 1½in (4cm) for the casing at the top of the hanging.

1 Cut out two main pieces of fabric to the overall dimensions, plus ¾in (2cm) all around for seam allowances. Also cut out each pocket, allowing an extra ½in (1.25cm) for seam allowances at the sides and bottom, and ¾in (2cm) at the top. Cut the dowel so that it is 4in (10cm) longer than the finished width of the catchall.

2 Cut out a piece of fusible interfacing the same size as the main fabric pieces excluding seam allowances. Iron it onto the back of one fabric piece.

3 Lay the other main fabric piece on top of the interfaced piece, right sides together. Stitch across the top and bottom, taking a ½in (1.25cm) seam and leaving a 8in (20.5cm) opening on one edge. Stitch the same size seam down both sides, leaving the top ¾in

(2cm) of the side seams open just below the top seam.

4 Trim the seams and corners, turn right side out, and press. Slipstitch the

opening closed. Topstitch ¾in (2cm) from the top edge to form a casing for the dowel.

5 Cut out the pieces of fabric for the pocket decoration, turn under a ⅛in (3mm) hem on each edge and press. Attach the decoration to each pocket by topstitching close to the edges.

6 Press under ¼in (6mm) then ½in (1.25cm) on top edge of each pocket; stitch. Press under ½in (1.25cm) on the side and bottom edges.

7 Pin all the pockets onto the interfaced side of the catchall, forming

two pleats on the bottom edge of each. Topstitch around the side and bottom edges of each pocket.

8 Slot the dowel through the casing at the top so that the ends extend beyond the side edges by 2in (5cm). Hang the catchall from hooks screwed into the wall on either side.

THE LITTLE PRINCESS'S ROOM

Our Little Princess's room has been inspired by the clean lines of traditional Scandinavian design, especially the beautiful nineteenth-century watercolors by Carl Larsson of his own daughter's bedroom at his home in Sweden. The Little Princess's room was designed to satisfy a young girl's yearning for a totally pink room (without having to make it so pink that she would grow out of it in a year). The fresh-looking checks and small floral prints make a classic combination in subtle pink tones, without being too sugary sweet.

The idea of an enclosed bed incorporating some storage space is irresistible to most young girls. Here, we echoed the bed skirt with the window treatment. The floorboards were painted white in order to keep the room bright, while the painted furniture insures that the bedroom remains feminine.

The furnishings are recreated in miniature inside the dolls' house – a project a young girl might enjoy doing herself, while at the same time learning basic sewing skills.

Very feminine but not overdone, this delicately decorated Little Princess's Bedroom is the epitome of many young girls' aspirations. Soft shades of rose pink, cozy corners, and pretty painted furniture almost belong to another age, and combine to form a timeless scheme for a little girl's fairy tale room. Scallop-edged valances set off the curtains on both the window and the bed.

STENCILED WALLPAPER BORDER

This fine scroll-design border has a faded elegance born of its soft blue-green, salmon-pink, and biscuit color combination. Stenciled onto lining paper (a plain paper sometimes used under wallpaper) whose texture is slightly uneven, it is a perfect finishing touch.

1 Unroll the paper and cut to a depth of about 12in (30cm) and a length of about 10ft (3m).

2 Trace the template at the back of the book, and transfer to stencil card or acetate. Cut out the stencil. Use low-tack masking tape to stick the stencil to the lining paper. First stencil in sky blue paint sparingly all along the length of the border. Leave the paint to dry, then replace the stencil in each position and apply blue-green paint sparingly. Stenciling all one color and then replacing the stencil, rather than doing both colors before repositioning it, creates an attractive, slightly out-of-register effect, adding an interesting softness to the edges. You can accentuate the effect by using a sponge rather than a brush to apply the paint, giving a dappled texture.

3 Draw a faint pencil line 1in (2.5cm) in from the top and bottom edges. (Or use low-tack masking tape to help you paint straight, but peel it off carefully.) Paint on the pink color with a flat 1in (2.5cm) wide brush. Seal the border with a flat latex glaze.

4 To mount the border, apply border paste, folding the paper accordion-fashion, then stick to the wall.

PAINTED DECORATION

By the age of about eight, girls have usually developed a fascination with dressing tables, and this painted wooden one has the requisite prettiness without the frills and flounces. The hand-painted decoration echoes the scroll pattern and the pink/green colors of the wallpaper border.

These subtle decorative extras, with their soft colors echoed in the stenciled border running around the walls of the room, provide a pleasing harmony with the off-white painted floorboards – clean, fresh and simple as only Scandinavian style can be.

Subtle pink scrolls are also painted onto the wardrobe door (left), whose panels feature a children's novelty print wallpaper, pasted on with white craft glue. The white background of the paper blends with the white door, making the images resemble hand-painting.

Another method of achieving a hand-painted look without actually having to draw was used on the small cupboard next to the fireplace (opposite). The characters were traced from children's illustrations and enlarged on a photocopier; the outlines were then transferred to the panels of the cupboard and painted in by hand.

An even easier method was used on the fireplace itself: photocopies of the figures were simply cut out and stuck onto the panels then hand-painted and sealed with a flat latex glaze.

The decoration was applied over a dusky pink glazed finish edged with soft blue-green on the fireplace, and over shades of biscuit framed by Gustavian blue and ice pink on the cupboard. For a translucent glaze such as this, dilute water-based paint until it gives only a light tracing of color on your chosen surface. Apply more than one coat if necessary.

DOLLS' HOUSE

Dolls' houses have an enduring and fascinating charm. Their miniature worlds provide endless possibilities for everyone, from three-year-olds to adults. Unlike real homes, the rooms can be redecorated as often as you like. A child can have fun reupholstering a sofa, changing the window coverings, or replacing the wallpaper – and will be able to complete it before they grow tired of the job. The furnishings can echo those of their own bedroom, as here, or else be completely different in style.

Make tiny cushions and bolsters and stuff them with cotton. Hang "proper" curtains (fringing the lower edges by removing a few horizontal threads) then hold them back with tiebacks made from narrow ribbon. Cut little bedcovers from fabric bearing motifs of the right scale. Use pinking shears to cut out gingham tablecloths.

SCALLOPED VALANCE, CURTAINS, & TIEBACKS

These simple curtains and coordinating scallop-edged valance lend an air of quiet sophistication to a young girl's room. The curtains are unlined to allow the light to filter through, adding to the airiness of the room. The scalloped edge of the valance can be piped or left plain. Combined with matching tiebacks, the sleek and tailored valance adds a smart informality to the room.

YOU WILL NEED

FABRIC FOR CURTAINS
FABRIC FOR VALANCE AND TIEBACKS
PLAIN FABRIC OR BIAS BINDING FOR CORDING
MATCHING SEWING THREAD
PIPING CORD
SELF-STYLING CURTAIN TAPE
FUSIBLE INTERFACING
SEW-AND-STICK VELCRO®
4 BRASS RINGS
2 HOOKS

MEASURING

Curtains

The fullness of the curtains will depend upon the self-styling tape you choose. Shirring tape requires 1½ to 2 times the width, pinch pleat tape 2 times and pencil pleat tape 3 times the width. Therefore, for the width of the curtains, multiply this number times the width of the rod, plus 3in (7.5cm) for the side hems. Divide this figure by the width of the fabric, and round up to get the number of fabric widths you will need.

For the length of each drop of the curtain fabric, measure from the rod to the desired length and add the depth of the tape plus 5in (12.5cm) for the bottom hem.

For the total amount of fabric you'll need, multiply the length of each drop by the number of widths. If the fabric is patterned, add the depth of one extra pattern repeat per fabric width after the first width.

Valance

For the fusible web, measure the width of your valance shelf (including the distance around the ends if you wish the valance to continue around the corners), and add 1in (2.5cm) for seam allowances. The depth of the valance is up to you, but the finished length of valances like this is generally about one-sixth the length of the curtains. Your valance fabric needs to be this depth plus 1in (2.5cm). Cut two pieces of fabric to these dimensions.

Tiebacks

To decide the length of your tiebacks, hold a tape measure around the curtain when it is pulled back. Add 1in (2.5cm) to this length for seam allowances. Experiment with the height. Sometimes tiebacks are fixed about two-thirds of the way down the curtain, other times fairly high up.

Curtains

1 Cut out enough fabric widths for each curtain, matching any pattern all the way across. Join the widths, right sides together, taking ½in (1.25cm) seams and matching the pattern. If your window requires an odd number of fabric widths, use a half width on each curtain and position it on the outside edge rather than the leading (inside) edge.

2 Press under ¼in (5mm) and then 2¾in (7cm) on each side edge. Stitch. Measure the depth of your self-styling tape and turn down this amount at the top; press.

3 Position the tape on the wrong side just inside the folded top edge. Knot the two cords together on the leading edge of each curtain and turn under

the end of the tape. Stitch across the end and along both edges, stitching in the same direction each time. At the outside edge, turn under the end of the tape, and stitch, being careful to keep the cords free.

4 On the bottom edge, turn under ¼in (5mm) and then 4¾in (12cm). Hand sew the hem in place.

5 Pull up the cords on the self-styling tape to form narrow pleats. When the curtain is the correct width, knot the cords together. (Do not cut them off.) Insert hooks behind each pleat, and hang from the rod.

Valance

1 If you do not already have a valance shelf, fit one 2–3in (5–8cm) above the window frame so it projects 2in (5cm) beyond each end of the curtain rod.

2 Cut a strip of fusible interfacing to the dimensions of the valance fabric excluding the seam allowances. Following the manufacturer's directions, iron the fusible interfacing to the wrong side of one fabric piece, along one edge.

3 Place the interfaced fabric on a flat surface, interfacing side facing up. Draw around a plate to create a scalloped edge ⅜in (1cm) inside the lower edge, leaving a gap of ⅜in (1cm) at each end. Also leave a gap of this size between semicircles if you plan to pipe the edge. Hand baste along the

marked line so the scalloped line will be visible from the right side.

4 If you are using fabric rather than purchased bias binding for the piping, cut strips of the plain fabric on the bias. (Work out the width the strips should be by wrapping the fabric around the piping cord and pinning it next to the cord. Add two ⅜in (1cm) seam allowances to this distance.) Join the ends of the bias strips on the straight grain, then wrap the binding around the piping cord. Baste the binding close to the cord.

5 Pin the piping along the basted scalloped line on the right side of the fabric, as shown, clipping into the seam allowances on the curves. Baste.

Place the other piece of fabric on top, right sides together, sandwiching the piping between. Stitch along the scalloped line, continuing across each end with a ⅜in (1cm) seam. Trim the seams and corners. Turn right side out and press. Turn in ⅜in (1cm) on the raw edges at the top; press and baste.

6 Stitch the sew-on side of the Velcro® along the top edge of the valance at the back. Remove the basting. Stick the self-adhesive side of the Velcro® to the valance shelf. Attach the valance.

Tiebacks

1 To draw up a crescent-shaped pattern, mark on a piece of paper a strip that is half the tieback length measurement by 4in (10cm) wide. Curve both sides at the bottom so that one end is narrowed to 1½in (4cm). Cut out this pattern.

2 Fold a piece of fabric in half on the straight grain and place the wide end of the pattern against the fold. Cut out, adding a ½in (1.25cm) seam allowance on the cut edges. Repeat for a second piece of fabric, but in reverse. Cut two more fabric pieces in the same way for the other tieback.

3 Using the template you have made, cut out a piece of fusible stiff inter-facing for each tieback, omitting the seam allowance. Fuse each to the wrong side of one fabric piece.

4 Make piping as for the valance (step 4), and baste all around the seamline on the right side of one tieback.

5 With right sides together, join the two fabric pieces, taking a ½in (1.25cm) seam and leaving an opening. Trim the seam, turn right side out, and press. Slipstitch the opening. Repeat for the other tieback.

6 Blanket stitch a ring in the center of each end on the wrong side so that it projects slightly beyond the fabric. Hook each tieback's pair of rings onto a hook on the wall.

BED HANGINGS

This delightful four-poster bed is a retreat and a reading area rolled into one. The bed frame, which simply slots over a divan bed, is made in much the same way as the bed frame on page 56 (and, like it, requires carpentry skills), but a fiberboard ceiling is added to the top and lined with fabric. After the bed frame has been constructed, the integral shelf unit is slipped into one end and screwed on. The outer curtains are hooked onto a rod attached to the frame so that they can be fully opened and closed. The valance is attached with Velcro® to a strip of hardboard fixed in front of the curtain rod.

Make the two outer curtains as for the window curtains. For the inner curtains, join enough widths to make one very wide curtain that will cover the wall on the far side and at the end behind the headboard. Stitch adhesive-backed self-styling curtain tape to the top, remove the backing, and stick to the bed frame. Make the valance as for the window valance, trimming the scalloped edge with piping if you wish.

The skirt around the bed (see page 82) incorporates a single inverted pleat, creating a tailored look that complements the gathered window curtains in the same striped fabric.

CHAPTER SIX

The Teenage Years

When children enter the teenage years, their increased awareness of themselves and their surroundings may mean that you have very little say in the decoration of their rooms, other than to provide financial support for furnishings.

You can help smooth the transition from child to young adult by allowing a teenager's room to reflect their own interests and personality. If all they want to do is lie around drinking coffee and strumming a guitar instead of indulging in regular exercise, then let them create a room that is a comfortable place to retreat to when the going gets tough. Since teenagers, when at home, spend much more time in their own rooms than younger children do, their space should really be their own.

For studious types, a built-in desk with fabric curtains to hide homework would be ideal, while sporty types would find a tall cupboard for sports equipment essential. Suggest rather than impose decorative changes, but be on hand to help out when required. If your offspring suddenly develop a passion for sewing, painting, woodwork, or metalwork, take care not to shun the creative urge for fear of a few gouges out of the wall, a paint-spattered floor, or a damaged sewing machine. Enthusiasm is all at this age.

A den that can be treated as a home within a home is the kind of room to which most teenagers aspire, and our Teenage Den (see page 97) provides a space they can call their own (and no doubt retire to at every available opportunity). Clothes, books, sports equipment, and home entertainment systems are all squeezed into this canopied room.

THE IDEAL BEDROOM

For most teenagers, the perfect bedroom would include furniture, equipment, and furnishings reminiscent of a studio apartment. It would be spacious, with not too much cumbersome furniture, but with plenty of improvised pieces to house equipment such as a computer, a stereo system, and vast quantities of CDs and tapes, a work desk and some musical instruments.

For entertaining friends, young adults need a social space away from the rest of the family. Their beds are not so much beds as communal daybeds, strewn with pillows, while sofas and armchairs can be draped with throws (and also, quite possibly, the contents of the closet, which can often be found spread over all available surfaces).

FURNITURE NEEDS

Whereas a busy 12-year-old will relish an organized, modular desk area plus shelves, a 16-year-old may well wish to demonstrate their independence by finding a battered storage cabinet in a junkyard and transforming it into a mobile TV trolley by painting it and replacing

the door. While an active 10-year-old will enjoy having tennis rackets and baseball bats neatly stacked in a cupboard or under the bed, an older teenager is more likely to toss them carelessly into whichever large receptacle is nearest the door.

Plan for this dramatic transition by investing in a few large containers such as wicker baskets, an aluminum waste basket, large wall-mounted shelves, or additional chests of drawers. Leave them unpainted, or strip existing pieces whose colors may now be inappropriate, and let your teenager decide on a color scheme. This way you cannot be blamed for a "boring" result – although you will undoubtedly be enlisted into a color-altering operation if anything does not turn out as planned.

Informal Indian fabrics and rich chenilles on scatter pillows and at the window add to the atmosphere of our Teenage Den (see pages 93 and 97). With a television as a focal point, this is certainly no homework corner.

An easy chair, enlivened with generous, bold-patterned pillows, can provide a focal point for the room's decoration. If the ceilings are high and strong, a hammock suspended from sturdy metal hooks fixed to a joist is an ideal place for teenage daydreaming and future-planning, offering a great escape from the work desk and exam pressures.

Define a social area by placing floor pillows on top of painted wooden pallets to form a low platform. Range them around a low coffee table piled with magazines and candles for the ultimate in teenager entertaining.

A kettle and some mugs hanging on hooks can form a mini kitchen. Separate it from the work or sleep area by a wicker screen.

If the size of the room dictates that there is space only for a bed, try removing the headboard and converting the sleeping area into a daybed/sofa by piling it high with large pillows, generous bolsters, and drapes and throws. Attach a simple canopy above it for an enclosed effect. Positioning it in an alcove will also help it to not look like a bed.

Provide an ample-sized desk for homework. It can even be improvised from a door placed on two trestles, which will allow some flexibility in the layout of the room. Bulletin boards are still important; repaint existing ones, or devote the upper half of one wall to a strip of corkboard. Make sure that the computer is placed away from direct light so that there is no problem with glare. Lighting should be localized and effective for late-night studying.

DECORATING

Children of this age will certainly be capable of performing nearly any decorating task. Persuading them that it will be fun to do may be more tricky. However, spur on their enthusiasm with a shopping trip to select fabric and accessories. Discuss ideas for making the room more of a space for one-room living than a bedroom.

Floor pillows are a good starting point for a decorating scheme. Choosing fabric for these may lead to some bold ideas for window treatments and bed linen elsewhere in the room. A fabric-covered wardrobe, which will house baseball bats, tennis rackets, and oars as well as a large amount of clutter, is another opportunity for a swath of bold color. While a traditional floral chintz may be spurned during the teenage years, a rich purple or burgundy plain fabric, jazzed up with checked or stripy floor pillows, would look dramatic and be well received.

Fabric can be used in bed hangings, too. Girls may prefer a bed canopy or a mock four-poster for a hint of romance: white muslin or plain damask would both work well.

Wallpaper is now appropriate, as it is less likely to be scuffed and marked. A pretty border with a vivid striped wallpaper, or a combination of dark colors and a subtle border, would suit a girl or a boy respectively, although girls may also prefer richer, deeper colors, for an atmosphere more like a study.

STORAGE

Teenagers tend to accumulate clutter of a different sort from younger children. Rather than toys and their tiny components, there will be plenty of paper to store. Notebooks of poems, looseleaf binders crammed with school notes and projects, textbooks and reference works will all need homes. Bookshelves are often far too small, having seemingly been designed for nothing but paperbacks. Try altering any existing wall-mounted shelves or consider devoting an entire wall to deep, open shelves. Make a virtue of larger items such as book bags and sports equipment, displaying them boldly atop shelves or in a sturdy fisherman's net suspended from the ceiling or a strong metal wall peg.

Whereas you may have gotten away with a small closet and a chest of drawers for clothes storage up to now, the teenage years usually mark a dramatic increase in the quantity of clothes, be they diaphanous dresses, myriad pairs of rugged, aged jeans, or volumes of T-shirts.

Consider investing in a large, freestanding wardrobe, or adapt any existing pigeonholes to house folded clothes.

As well as the fabric-covered wardrobe already mentioned, which can hold large amounts of clutter in a relatively small space, another option is a trunk on castors – it can double as clothes storage and a low table.

A change in a room's layout can often mark the transition from one stage of childhood to the next. One way of providing extra storage is to move the bed into the center of the room and create a mock headboard by arranging four chests of drawers or cupboards around it in a U-shape. This not only encloses the bed but also provides walk-around storage and a surface for table lamps, decorative pieces, and piles of reading matter. Or place the bed against the back of a freestanding wardrobe, creating a walk-in dressing area behind the bed rather than devoting a whole wall to a built-in closet.

DETAILS

Mirrors play an important part in the lives of teenagers, so make a feature of them and place them in prominent positions. Contact paper can be used to cover plain wooden frames, or frames can be painted to match bulletin boards or woodwork elsewhere in the room. Surround the mirror with pegs on which brushes, combs, hair dryers, and jewelry can be displayed and stored. This minimizes the effort involved in keeping the room tidy. Laundry also becomes important to a teenager – or at least having somewhere to put clothes ready for the wash does. Provide a deep laundry hamper or metal waste basket, depending on the style of room. Confine it to a corner, possibly disguised with a screen, and empty it when necessary. Your progeny certainly won't remember to, unless desperate for something to do.

THE TEENAGER'S BEDROOM: FURNISHING SUGGESTIONS

Bed, possibly with storage underneath	Home entertainment/stereo/TV storage
Large wardrobe or built-in storage for clothes	Accent pillows and low table
Well-lit study desk	Futon or daybed with throws
Shelves for school files	Coat-rack and hooks
Table/work station for computer	Large bulletin board

THE TEENAGE DEN

For those years when children are becoming young adults, a flexible approach to furnishing is called for. Our Teenage Den (shown on pages 92–93) is the sort of room teenagers would themselves choose. The fabric is inexpensive, and it is arranged over the bed and at the window in quick, easy to hang ways designed for maximum impact with minimum effort.

SIMPLE WINDOW TREATMENTS

Lengths of plain cheesecloth in vibrant shades of Kashmir red and saffron yellow are pinned with strong thumbtacks to the window frames of our Teenage Den, one overlapping the other so that they give the sunlight streaming through them a summery glow even on the coldest of days. Here, they are both pulled back on one side with wrought-iron holdbacks.

Another way to create an informal effect is to drape layers of cheesecloth in different colors or a mixture of plain and patterned fabrics over a metal or wooden pole. They can be finished off with a fabric bow tieback, a tassel, or a cord. Or tie a single cheesecloth curtain to a pole in a variation of our Amazon curtains (page 64) and gather in the middle with a huge cheesecloth sash.

SMART IMPROVISATION

An airy, informal arrangement of furniture and fabric makes this room seem as if anything can happen with the decoration. The bed canopy is easily replaceable or movable, as are the window treatments, which are simply pinned on, and the headboard, which is on castors.

Note the cheap, secondhand metal cabinet, easily painted by the teenager, and perfect for storing sports equipment. The low futon bed, with its colorful bedspread and bolster, can double as an ethnic sofa.

BED CANOPY

To make a simple bed canopy like the one on the left, take a length of lightweight fabric that complements the bed covering. Hem each long edge (unless it is on the selvage) and both ends. Insert two screw eyes into the ceiling above where each end of the canopy will be, and run a length of sturdy wire between each pair of screw eyes. Now simply drape the fabric over the two wires. Knot the draped ends or attach fringe, braid, or contrasting binding. To coordinate the look, use the same fabric for bolster or pillow covers or for binding the edges of curtains.

DECORATING THE BED

In teenagers' rooms, because the bed will often double as a daytime and evening lounging area, it's much appreciated if you make it comfortable by adding generous bolsters, soft oversized pillows, and interesting throws.

Some kind of canopy or enclosure will increase the sense of privacy, so you might consider constructing a more adult version of the bedframe in the Owl and the Pussycat Bedroom (see page 55). Instead of making a wooden punched cornice, drape the horizontal pieces with lengths of fabric, or make curtains with tab or eyelet headings. The more fabric you use, the more lavish the look will be.

HEADBOARD WITH STORAGE

Customized furniture is one way of accommodating the teenager's love of informality while still allowing for some decoration. The bed in our Teenage Den (see pages 98–99), with its L-shaped headboard, is particularly versatile, because it can be positioned as it has been there, like an island, or it can be placed with the other side of the bed up against a wall.

The headboard is simple to construct using two existing pieces of bedroom furniture: a chest of drawers and a deep cupboard. Placed with the storage areas facing outward, they are held together with thin fiberboard or plywood screwed to the L-shaped top. To link them visually, more fiberboard or plywood is attached to each of the inward-facing vertical surfaces. Mounting castors on each corner of the underside allows the whole unit to be moved.

Paint the fiberboard or plywood and, if you wish, decorate it with stenciling, decoupage, or stamping techniques.

Alternatively, for a softer effect, drape the unit with fabric and simply pile boxes covered in a coordinating fabric on top of it.

FUTON

Futons are popular with teenagers, either to sleep on themselves or to use as spare beds. Adults, it must be said, often cannot understand what the attraction is, as futons do tend to be less soft than conventional beds, and take some getting used to. These firm mattresses can be supported on a low, slatted wood base, as here, or used on the floor and then rolled up during the day. When the mattress is rolled up halfway, the built-in backrest makes it an ideal spot for relaxing. This futon, which is about 4in (10cm) thick, is made from upholstery batting (available from upholsterers) and is hand-tufted at regular intervals.

YOU WILL NEED

COTTON FABRIC

MATCHING SEWING THREAD

1IN (2.5CM) THICK UPHOLSTERY BATTING

UPHOLSTERER'S NEEDLE

TWINE

1 Cut out two pieces of fabric to the desired length of the futon plus 3½in (9cm) and the desired width plus 3½in (9cm). Cut four layers of batting, each to the desired dimensions (without adding extra).

2 The fabric covering is made first. With right sides together, join both long edges with ¾in (2cm) seams but leave a central opening in one of these seams for most of the length.

3 Refold the fabric so the seams run down the center of each side, then stitch a ¾in (2cm) seam across each end. Press the seams open.

4 At each corner, separate the front and back, centering the seam. Mark a 4in (10cm) long line across the corner, pin, and stitch through both layers. Do not trim the seam. When all four corners have been stitched, turn the cover right side out.

5 Insert the layers of batting through the center back opening. Slipstitch the opening closed, using a double length of thread and placing the stitches very close together.

6 Mark the positions of the tufts so they are about 10in (25cm) apart, and staggered. Thread the upholsterer's needle with a double or quadruple length of twine. Take the needle through from front to back, leaving 4in (10cm) long ends. Bring the needle back to the front, to make a 1in (2.5cm) wide stitch. Tie the ends of twine in a firm square knot, then trim them to 2½in (6.5cm).

BOLSTERS

YOU WILL NEED

BOLSTER FORM
FABRIC
MATCHING THREAD
ZIPPER, ABOUT ¾ THE LENGTH OF THE
BOLSTER

Long bolsters are ideal for relaxing on, whether used on a low bed or futon, or combined with pillows of other shapes and sizes. The long lines of the bolster mean that striped fabrics are especially suitable. If the stripe or pattern is quite strong, a tailored bolster with a zipper, like the one shown on pages 98–99, generally works best. If you prefer it to be a little less plain, you can pipe the ends.

1 Cut a piece of fabric as long as the bolster plus 1½in (4cm), and as wide as the circumference of the bolster plus 1½in (4cm). Cut two circles from the fabric, with the diameter of each equal to the diameter of the bolster plus 1½in (4cm).

2 With right sides together, fold the fabric in half and stitch along the length, taking a ¾in (2cm) seam but

machine basting rather than stitching where the zipper will be inserted. Insert the zipper, then remove the basting and open the zipper.

3 With right sides together, pin each end to a circle. Stitch, taking a ¾in (2cm) seam and clipping into the seam allowance on the curves. Turn right side out through the zipper opening and insert the bolster form.

STUDY AREA

Make homework more appealing by paying some attention to the study area. Create a good-sized desk using simple trestles with a door laid on top. Site it next to some equally functional, no-nonsense shelving. Or, for a less streamlined look, disguise cluttered open shelves with fabric drapes, and add comfort to work chairs with cushions. Decorate simple cork bulletin boards with painted borders or fabric edging.

If there is a television, incorporate it into the room by placing it on a fabric-draped low table, or fit it on a swivel arm so it can "disappear" into a curtained alcove when study time takes over. Surround it with floor pillows for informal viewing.

CHAPTER SEVEN

Beyond the Bedroom

T he presence of children in a home should be celebrated rather than disguised, although their propensity to spread toys, belongings, and friends to all corners of the dwelling can be alarming for those of an orderly tendency.

Once their bedrooms become their havens, children like to use other parts of the house – and yard – for different activities. It is a good idea to anticipate which spaces will become dens, entertainment areas, or lounging-around sites and plan them accordingly. Children love nothing better than cozy nooks and crannies in which to hide or indulge their imaginations with make-believe.

By devoting another space in the house to children's activities you will create an additional gathering place which will relieve pressure on other busy parts of the home. It should also enable you to preserve at least one room that is strictly for the grown-ups.

If you are short of additional space, think about providing an extra play area, seating, or storage under the stairs, in an underused alcove, in the hallway, or on the landing. Use room dividers in a large room to separate off a toy storage space for youngsters or a leisure area for older children.

Outside, there is often considerable scope for coping with overflow from indoors. Garden sheds, sunporches, or conservatories added onto the side of the house and freestanding playhouses are all ways of making room for children.

A playroom can be conjured up from any available space in the home – off a kitchen or living room is ideal. In our Creative Playroom (page 110) an open doorway has been transformed into a puppet theater, while a wigwam provides a place to hide or a special location for indoor picnics.

OUTDOORS

Playhouses, rope ladders and swings, sandboxes, miniature gardens, and wading pools are all an intrinsic part of childhood. Treehouses are the scene of many a secret assignment planned during lunchtime picnics, where flashlights and binoculars, spy notebooks and bird-spotting are de rigueur.

Playhouses in whatever form are even more fun in the garden than indoors. The wigwam in our Creative Playroom (page 110) can be set up anywhere, inside or out. Or create a canopied den by draping fabric over beanpoles; bold florals will conjure up a country garden, and stripy canvas a sense of the seaside.

A shed could double as a playhouse: stow away all dangerous equipment and put pretty gingham curtains with bow tiebacks on the windows. Add a couple of wicker hampers and a cane chair for a pastoral hideaway your children will remember forever.

KITCHENS

Preschool children, especially, love being around you in the kitchen. It's generally when you are preparing for company that they want to embark on an epic artwork involving the entire contents of the crafts cupboard and a few discarded household items. With a large table and the right equipment, you will be able to continue the preparations while keeping a supervisory eye on their artistic endeavors.

Now that the kitchen is one of the most lived-in rooms of the home, it makes sense to devote some space here to children's activities. It is safest if the cooking and food-preparation part of the kitchen is placed at one end, or in one corner, while a table for meals and other practical pursuits is at the other end. Provide some form of toy storage, a miniature table and chairs, and "wet play" space for painting, working with play dough, and cutting and gluing collages. If you have a large window, consider building a window seat with a hinged lid to hide painting equipment and toys. Or construct some pigeonholes for toy and craft materials storage, and hang a fabric shade in front of it to disguise the contents.

However you organize the space when the children are young, it can be adapted as they grow. The same space can be given over to an easy chair and some books, a fold-down work desk and chair, or a home entertainment area complete with television and miniature stereo system on a swivel arm.

Encourage tidiness at an early age by providing child-height hooks and pegs for storing coats, hats, cardigans, and painting aprons.

A wigwam is a neat alternative to the more usual playhouse. It will inspire dressing-up games as well as making the transition from indoors to garden very easily.

LIVING ROOMS

However much you may wish to preserve the living room as the grown-up room of the house, children do tend to congregate here. If you decide that there really is nowhere else to accommodate additional toys and games, then there are ways of incorporating youthful possessions into the scheme of things without the room looking like an overstocked toy shop.

In the first place, store here only toys that will be played with in this room. Try dividing off a corner of the room with a fabric or wicker screen to hide baskets of toys and board games. Computers can be housed on a roll-out trolley in an armoire or built-in cupboard, along with children's video and cassette tapes. Store books on low shelves, within easy reach of children.

If the room is large enough, devote one end or one corner of the room to the children and demarcate it by painting it a different color or by pasting a border at chair rail height. Alternatively, screen off the area with curtains or separate it with a screen, sofa, or table.

In a living room where all members of the family will inevitably gather, certain things are best avoided while children are young. Among them are cream or white sofas and carpets and glass-topped tables. Ceramics, antiques, and fine upholstery simply will not survive the energetic games of rambunctious five-year-olds. However strict you are about insisting on stockinged feet and banning food and drink from the living room, the very speed at which children charge around when they have friends over would make

breakages inevitable. It is far safer, for your blood pressure and peace of mind, to insure that sofas and chairs have slip covers, coffee tables are kept simple and uncluttered (and out of the way when toddlers are about), and lamps have their cords secured or hidden. Make sure treasured china is well out of reach, together with any other highly prized objects. Keep your Persian carpet or needlepoint upholstery for when the children have left home.

On the walls, pale color schemes will get dirty more quickly than rich colors. On windows, insure that your drapery rods are secure. Who doesn't remember having a quick swing on the drapes when the adults were out of the room?

There is something very reassuring about generously pleated drapes in a living room. Valances and tiebacks will lend an air of traditional domesticity. Checked throws will help protect sofas during the daytime rough-and-tumble; at night fold them up or drape them and enjoy pristine seating.

Dining chairs and an old rug make an excellent basis for a makeshift playhouse. Children invariably prefer imaginary games such as this to the latest fad board game, so try to be flexible if the younger generation wants to reorganize the layout of the room temporarily.

One advantage of being fairly relaxed about your furnishings is that you will not need to fret about anything valuable being ruined. And you will at least be guaranteed some peace while the living room is transformed into a Swiss Family Robinson home.

PLAYROOMS

If you have the space, creating a playroom out of one part of the kitchen, a small room off the living room, or a bedroom is an ideal way to allow children the freedom to spread out their toys and activities undisturbed by the rigors of routine. It will mean less space in their bedroom devoted to storage and, for families of two or more children, a place where the youngsters can gather together.

You don't need a massive home with lots of spare rooms. Any small room can be adapted as a playroom and can also incorporate other activities. If equipped with a sofa bed and chest of drawers it can double as a guest room. With a small desk and adequate task lighting it can also be used as a sewing room or study – especially useful if you have teenagers and young children at home. As an adjunct to a kitchen or in an underused dining room, a playroom forms an extension of the heart of the home and allows you to watch over small ones as they play and you get on with chores.

When decorating a playroom, avoid making the more permanent furnishings look too childish – especially if the room will double as a study or guest room.

If you supply childlike decor in the form of posters or soft toys suspended in mock hammocks, and stacking boxes or baskets filled with toys, then you can choose wall, window, and floor coverings that will appeal to all ages. However, avoid carpet if your children are quite young, and choose instead a large rug, placed over a nonslip mat.

An old chimneybreast in our Creative Playroom (pages 104–105 and overleaf) provides a cozy alcove for miniature furniture, while cupboards are painted in a harlequin style.

From a safety point of view, check that you have enough electrical outlets, so you can avoid dangling cords. Place some outlets midway up the wall if a computer is to be installed at some point. Protect outlets with child-proof covers.

A comfortable playroom is one that any member of the family will like to use for time out, while watching the little ones play, or chatting with teenagers about homework problems. It provides an extra family room where a range of activities can take place.

THE CREATIVE PLAYROOM

As every child knows, learning is fun when it is through creative play. This cheerful playroom (shown in full on pages 104–105) offers exactly that. Painted numbers and letters decorate the walls and playthings, and there is plenty of opportunity for stimulating activities, ranging from games and play-acting to stories and craft work. There is also ample storage, all of it attractive and colorful.

COLOR-BY-NUMBER WALLS

Letters and numbers are enormously interesting to children of this age. Not only are they of great value educationally, but they also have infinite decorative applications. You can stencil names onto walls or furniture, paint numbers directly onto a floor for an instant games area, or form a border at chair rail height on a wall.

Here, letters and numbers have been hand-painted more or less at random on the yellow colorwashed walls. Simply trace the letters and numerals at the back of the book, transfer the designs onto the walls, and then paint them in.

Or, if you aren't confident about hand-painting, use the templates to make stencils.

On one area of wall at the end of the room, we used a deeper yellow for the background, framing this with an even darker shade of yellow and a fine orange line. At the top, the numbers form a frieze. Defining a specific part of the wall in this way creates a large display area that is just right for those pictures proudly brought home from school.

To make the painted walls easy to clean, protect them with a flat latex glaze.

DIAMOND DESIGN CUPBOARDS

Abstract or geometric shapes combine well with letter and number motifs and have been used to decorate the cupboards in this playroom in various ways, all using diluted latex paint in blues and yellows.

On the wide cupboard door shown on the far right of the photograph above, the diamonds are created by first glazing the full panel in pale blue, then stenciling yellow diamond shapes on the raised central portion of each border. Stenciling with a sponge rather than a brush creates an uneven look that goes well with the

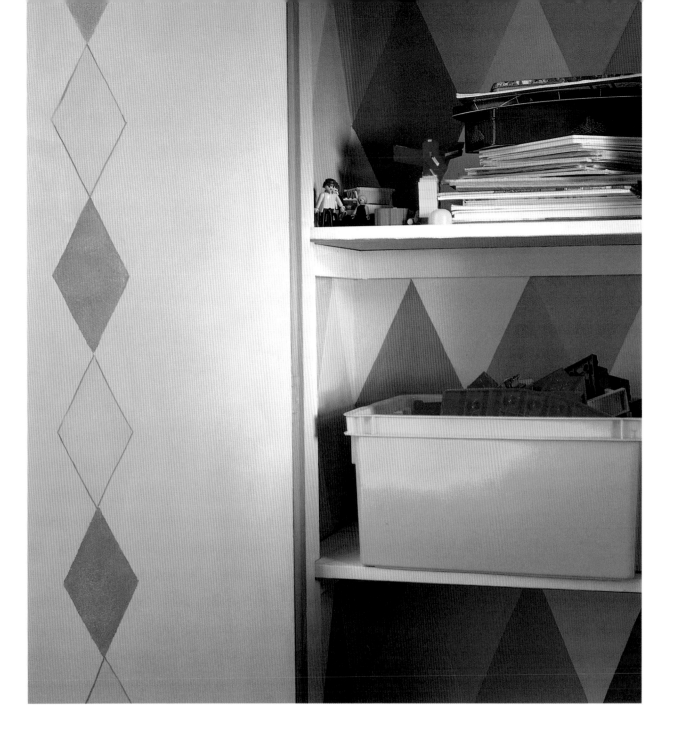

glazing. The trim is painted in the same pale blue, and everything is protected with a flat acrylic varnish.

On the narrow cupboard door shown on the left of the photograph on page 109, blue diamonds have been stenciled onto yellow panels, again using a sponge, with the moldings and the door frame picked out in blue.

The inside of the cupboard door, which is shown above, has been given a similar treatment, but alternate diamonds are stenciled (with a sponge) in a deeper yellow, then outlined by hand in blue, and varnished.

The inside of the cupboard itself has hand-painted harlequin diamonds which have been sealed with flat latex glaze.

WIGWAM

This wigwam can be used indoors or out and is just the place for a secret pow-wow, a quiet picnic, or private reading. Fairly simple to make, it will stimulate children's imaginations and quickly become a favorite plaything.

YOU WILL NEED

STRONG COTTON FABRIC SUCH AS CANVAS
OR UNBLEACHED MUSLIN

MATCHING SEWING THREAD

6 BAMBOO CANES,
EACH ABOUT 6FT 6IN (2M) LONG

¼IN (6MM) WIDE ROPE

¾IN (2CM) WIDE GROSGRAIN RIBBON

ACRYLIC PAINT

MEASURING

Assemble your canes and tie them together with a rope to form the basic wigwam structure. Measure the canes, adding 1in (2.5cm) for hems, and use this measurement as a radius for drawing a semicircle for the cover.

1 Tie a pencil to a piece of string the length of your radius. Hold the other end in place and use the string to draw a semicircle on newspaper; cut out the pattern. Join widths of fabric as necessary to make a large enough piece, then draw around the pattern and cut out the semicircle from fabric.

2 At the center of the straight edge, draw and cut out a semicircle large enough to fit around the top of the tied poles – probably about 6in (15cm) across. Turn under a ½in (1.25cm) double hem around the top and bottom edges, and also the side edges.

3 Paint, stencil, or stamp your chosen designs onto the canvas. Here we used children's hand prints and stenciled numbers and letters.

4 Place the canvas over the canes, with the front opening positioned centrally between two canes. One side will overlap the other.

5 Cut the ribbon into one piece 4in (10cm) long and 15 pieces about 12in (30cm) long. Cut three of the long pieces in half. Mark on the opening edges where the six halved ribbons will go; three should be sewn on the wrong side of the overlap, and the other three opposite them, on the right side of the underlap. Also mark the position of fabric ties at the bottom edge and halfway up each cane on the inside. Finally, mark the position for a loop on the outside, halfway up and about a

third of the way around, so the door flap can be tied back. The 4in (10cm) piece of ribbon will be used for this.

6 Remove the fabric from the canes and sew on the loop and the three pairs of short ribbons at the front. Fold the longer ribbons in half and sew the folded edge of each to the marked positions.

HOPSCOTCH FLOORCLOTH

Along with marbles, spinning tops, jumping rope, and leapfrog, hopscotch is one of those children's games that have remained popular for generations. Painting the squares on a floorcloth not only looks good, but it also allows the game to be enjoyed in the comfort of one's own playroom. Enlarge the numerals from the templates at the back of the book.

YOU WILL NEED

WHITE CANVAS FABRIC

1IN (2.5CM) WIDE WHITE OR TWILL TAPE

LOW-TACK MASKING TAPE

LATEX OR ACRYLIC PAINTS IN YELLOW AND THREE OTHER COLORS

ACRYLIC VARNISH

1 Cut a piece of canvas to the size you require and turn the raw edges to the front. Cover them with twill tape to form a border. Machine stitch around all edges to secure.

2 Use masking tape to protect the edging, then paint the whole canvas yellow. Leave to dry thoroughly.

Remove the masking tape and paint the twill tape in a contrasting color.

3 Measure and mark out the squares on the canvas. Enlarge the numerals and cut out from cardboard. Draw around these in the squares.

4 Remove the templates and paint around the number outlines within the squares using three different colors. Leave to dry thoroughly, then varnish.

WORLD MAP TOY CHEST

This unusual decoupage toy chest with painted decoration is dual-purpose, being both functional and educational. To make this toy chest, color photocopies of an antique map of the world were glued onto an old chest with white craft glue. Motifs such as fish and abstract shapes were then cut out of tissue paper, glued onto the maps, and painted, allowing the map to show through partially. Finally, the chest was given a protective coat of varnish.

PUPPET THEATER AND PUPPETS

Following a tradition that goes back centuries, this charming puppet theater is basically just a fabric panel that hangs in a doorway. A window cut into it, embellished with a zigzag valance and curtains, creates a stage for puppet shows that will provide hours of fun for children and the rest of the family. Because it hangs in a doorway, there will always be room for the puppeteers to slip behind it and perform. It is also easily portable and can therefore be used in different rooms in the house.

Either use puppets your children already have, or make simple ones from wooden spoons, as shown here. These are ideal for smaller children, who can grip the handles with ease. Encourage youngsters to paint on faces and to stick on hair. Children will also love helping to choose scraps of fabric for the clothes and will no doubt have ideas about colors and the style of clothes. Choose fabrics that reflect the character of the puppet – such as blue and white stripes for a pirate and shiny pink fabric for a princess.

YOU WILL NEED

THEATER
MAIN FABRIC, FOR THEATER PANEL
TWO CONTRASTING FABRICS, FOR CURTAINS AND TIEBACKS
MATCHING SEWING THREAD
1IN (2.5CM) WIDE TWILL TAPE
2 DOWELS
1IN (2.5CM) WIDE WOODEN SLAT
TENSION ROD, TO FIT IN DOORWAY

PUPPETS
2 LONG WOODEN SPOONS
FABRIC SCRAPS
MATCHING SEWING THREAD
FELT IN FLESH COLOR AND YELLOW
2 RUBBER BANDS
WATER-BASED PAINTS
WHITE CRAFT GLUE
YARN

Theater

1 Measure your doorway and add 6in (15.5cm) to both the width and the length. Cut out one piece of main fabric to these dimensions. Turn under ½in (1.25cm) and then 2½in (6.5cm) on both sides. Press and stitch.

2 Make a casing at the bottom by turning under ½in (1.25cm) and then 2½in (6.5cm), and stitching. Insert a wooden slat into it, cutting the slat to the width of the panel. Make a casing the same size at the top.

3 Cut a square hole in the curtain so that the sides are about 5in (13cm) from the hemmed edges. Make sure that the bottom edge of the window is higher than your children's heads but not so high that they cannot comfortably hold puppets up to it. Also check that it will be as tall as the puppets you will be using.

4 Clip diagonally into the corners for ¾in (2cm), and turn under a ⅝in (1.5cm) hem all around; stitch.

5 Attach a length of twill tape to the wrong side of the fabric along the lower edge of the window, stitching along both long edges. Cut one dowel to the window width and insert into the casing formed by the twill tape.

6 Cut two curtains from the contrasting fabric, each the depth of the window plus 5½in (14cm) by the width of the window. Stitch a double ⅜in (1cm) hem on each side and the bottom. At the top, turn under and stitch ¼in (6mm) then 1½in (4cm) to form a casing. Cut the remaining dowel so it is the width of the window plus 3in (7.5cm). Slot it into both casings, gathering the curtains onto it. Using thread loops, attach the dowel to the theater front, above the window.

7 Make a miniature zigzag valance as for the zigzag edging on page 56 and sew above the curtains.

8 For the tiebacks, cut two 5 x 30in (12.5 x 75cm) strips of another contrasting fabric and stitch together down both ends and the long side, leaving an opening and taking a ¼in (6mm) seam. Trim corners, turn right side out, and press. Slipstitch the opening. Tie one around each curtain.

9 Slot the tension rod through the casing at the top of the theater and mount in a doorway.

Puppets

1 Create two different-sized tunics for each puppet by cutting circles from the fabric scraps. Cut a smaller circle at the center point of the circle.

2 Cut four felt arm shapes for each puppet. Glue the arm shapes together in pairs and glue these arms onto the sides of each spoon. Paint a face on one side of each wooden spoon.

3 Using a double length of thread, hand sew gathering stitches around the central holes in each circle. Wrap a rubber band several times around the neck of the wooden spoon. Fit the tunic over the spoon and pull up the gathers to make a snug fit.

4 Tie scarves made from strips of fabric around the puppets' necks. For the hat, cut a piece of felt and twist it into shape. To make the puppet's hair, wrap yarn around a piece of cardboard 30–40 times. Slip the loops off the cardboard, tie them on one side, and cut the other side. Glue to the spoon, trimming the ends to shape.

CHAPTER EIGHT

Children's Bathrooms

A bathroom solely devoted to children may sound like an unnecessary luxury but, in fact, any bathroom that children will gravitate to without fuss at the end of a busy day makes good sense, as it is a treat for everyone. An inspiring and innovative theme to stimulate young ones' imaginations, combined with cheerful accessories and bath toys, will guarantee a calmer, more relaxed pre-bedtime for all concerned.

A separate space for the younger generation can often be devised with a little ingenuity. This will be particularly useful in larger families or where everyone needs to use the bathroom at the same time in the morning.

A child's bathroom need not include a bath or shower; even just a half-bath with a mirror and small storage area, fitted into a small space somewhere in the home, will help reduce morning traffic in the main bathroom.

Make sure that all safety requirements (see pages 121 and 130) are met, and never leave very young children unattended in the bathroom, even if they are with older siblings.

Bathtime is bound to be fun in a room such as our Deep Blue Sea Bathroom (see page 122) inhabited by myriads of deep-sea creatures. Bathed, cleaned, and dried amid an ocean scene, children will hopefully respond to the inspired decoration by peacefully complying with bedtime routines.

DECORATING

Even tiny spaces can be jollied up with bright fabric shades, delicate lace panels, or striped curtains in seaside colors. Deckchair canvas and traditional ticking are both ideal for a much-used bathroom as they not only look good but are tough and durable. Try making simple shades with them and attach them to the wall with candlewick string. Painted height charts and fun laundry hampers also brighten up the space.

An underwater theme is obviously highly appropriate for a bathroom and is great fun for children. The Deep Blue Sea Bathroom shown on pages 118–119, which is in fact used by all the family, is based on this watery theme. In addition to the fishy motifs that are featured in that bathroom, there are many other ways to introduce an aquatic element. For storing toys, make string bags look like fishing nets by tying or sewing on small shells, then fill them with tiny metal buckets and shovels, plastic ducks, and wooden fish for decorative effect. Use green nylon net to make a wall display, threading through small starfish, sea anemones, wooden sailing boats, and flotsam and jetsam. Edge a small wooden wall shelf with wave or fish shapes, and top it with wooden fish or seabirds, shells, and sponges.

Another theme that is easy to achieve in a bathroom is the classic combination of wood and wicker against a white backdrop. Painted wicker chairs with floral cushions soften an otherwise monochromatic scheme. Wooden slatted blinds at small windows can be softened by the addition of a simple valance above them.

Create a Mediterranean feel by painting and distressing wall cupboards and shelves in vivid blues and yellows, and complementing them with colorwashed walls and red, blue, and yellow fabrics in bold, painterly stripes or irregular checks. Combine them with brightly painted wooden toys displayed on a small shelf and bathtime will never seem dull.

SURFACE MAGIC

Tiles are the most obvious choice for bathroom walls. If you are putting up new tiles, look for designs and colors that bear out your theme – there are, for example, some lovely fish tiles.

Tongue-and-groove paneling is at once practical and appealing in a bathroom used predominantly by children. Protected with paint and/or varnish, it will withstand spills and also provide a background for a decorative backsplash. This can be painted, sponged, or stenciled with images that match the style of the room. Top with a narrow, lipped shelf for seashore paraphernalia and children's toiletries.

A splashboard, cut into a wavy shape with a jigsaw and decorated with colorful fish motifs, can be mounted straight onto a wall or, as in our Deep Blue Sea Bathroom (page 122), attached to existing tongue-and-groove paneling.

USING MOTIFS

If you feel confident about your painting skills, try painting a freehand frieze or a row of repeating motifs such as seaweed, stars, polkadots, or a wavy line. Otherwise, cut out simple shapes from magazines to use as templates for stencils; or photocopy then paint with water-based paint and stick them to the backsplash with white craft glue. Seal with varnish in order to make them waterproof.

Sponging is a supremely easy way of transferring images from one surface to another. Simple images without much detail are best for sponging. Just mark your chosen shape on a thick decorating sponge with a marker, cut out

the shape using an X-acto knife, take up some paint then use it to stamp the images. This is simple enough that children can help with it too.

Underwater images can be created by painting freehand, stenciling, sponging, or stamping. Let children help so they can sit in the bath and admire their handiwork.

STORAGE

Bathroom cabinets are also very simple to make or decorate. Use a piece of junk shop furniture to create a stylized cupboard decorated with fish and shells, or use rough, old floorboards to make a driftwood-style cabinet, complete with antique door lock, huge metal key, and candlewick string as a door pull. Build in a mirror to the inside of the door, or at the front.

Storing bath toys in a small space calls for a touch of ingenuity. A good solution is to use a dual-purpose container such as a wooden box on castors which can double as a small seat. A strong, lidded wicker chest would serve just as well. Alternatively, freestanding open metal shelves will store towels and toiletries at the top and bathroom toys below.

SAFETY CONSIDERATIONS

Safety is important in a children's bathroom. Make sure that the flooring is a nonslip, wipe-clean material such as cork or linoleum. Any rugs should be placed on a nonslip mat or have a

nonslip backing. Use a sturdy step for smaller children to reach the sink. Store all medicines in a lockable cabinet, out of reach. See page 130 for more information on bathroom safety.

THE DEEP BLUE SEA BATHROOM

Our children's bathroom (shown on pages 118–19) was inspired by the glorious blues of the ocean and the infinite variety of sea life. Get children to help choose fishy accessories for the bath and appropriate towels. They will feel awfully important when showing friends the way to "their" bathroom.

BATH BACKSPLASH

An inviting backdrop for reluctant bathers, this splendid underwater scene is applied to painted fiberboard by means of sponge-prints, stencils, and freehand painting. Children can help with the sponging, as it is as simple as potato printing. The motifs, many of which have templates at the back of the book, echo those on the fabric window shade. Screwed onto existing paneling with cross-head screws, a backsplash like this can be easily removed for a revamp or a different story.

YOU WILL NEED

FIBERBOARD

JIGSAW

LATEX PAINT IN DEEP BLUE

ACRYLIC PAINTS IN A VARIETY OF COLORS

SPONGES, STENCILS, AND PAINTBRUSHES

FLAT ACRYLIC VARNISH

1 Draw wave shapes on the sheets of fiberboard and cut out the outlines with a jigsaw. Sand the edges smooth. Paint the fiberboard with latex paint in deep blue for the background.

2 Apply the fish and plant motifs by a variety of methods. Cut fish shapes from sponges and coat these with a thin layer of acrylic paint. Stencil some motifs in one or two colors, using stencil brushes or sponges to apply the paint through the stencil. Detailing such as eyes can be hand-painted, and you can also paint whole motifs freehand if you wish.

3 Apply a couple of coats of flat acrylic varnish to protect the surface, allowing it to dry between coats.

TROPICAL FISH CABINET

Painted decoration transforms an old junk shop cupboard into a children's bathroom cabinet that is both fanciful and functional. The contrasting textures of the distressed surface, the background colors, and the tropical fish and shells all add to its appeal.

The cabinet has been decorated using diluted latex paints for a faded, watery finish, though the uneven, rough texture of the background is achieved by painting the diluted water-based paint over an oil base in a deeper color. The waves and bubbles are added with diluted white latex paint. The distinctive translucency and texture of the tropical fish and shells are created by gluing tissue paper shapes onto the cabinet with white craft glue and then painting them. Finally, the cabinet is varnished to protect it from the damp environment.

PAINTED DECORATION

Paneled doors and wooden bathroom furniture offer surfaces tailormade for underwater motifs. For this cupboard door, pale blue water-based paint was watered down to create a dilute texture and broken surface. The orange fish were created by cutting out sponge shapes and coating them with a layer of orange paint before stamping them on rather like potato prints. The purple fish were applied using a stencil. Finally, the decoration was sealed with a flat acrylic varnish. The table was painted with a wave-motif edging to echo the backsplash.

HEIGHT CHART

Children love checking how much they have grown, and a height chart on the bathroom wall is a splendid way to involve them in decorating the room. This one has been painted onto a strip of plain lining paper trimmed to fit the tongue-and-groove matchboarding, but you could mount the painted paper on a plain wall, or paint straight onto paneling. The painting technique and motifs are the same as for the Bath Backsplash (see page 122), with each measurement painted onto a bubble.

DRAWSTRING BAGS

Fabric bags hanging from hooks provide a handy place to keep children's bathroom toys and supplies. For each bag, cut out a rectangle and fold it in half crosswise, right sides together. Stitch down one side and across the end, leaving a ¾in (2cm) opening in the side seam starting 5in (13cm) from the top. Trim the corners, turn right side out, and press. Turn under ¼in (6mm) and then 3in (7.5cm) on the top edge and stitch. Stitch again, 1¾in (4.5cm) from the top edge.

Make up a narrow fabric tie by cutting a 1½in (4cm) wide strip of the same fabric, folding the long raw edges to nearly meet at the center and then folding it in half lengthwise. Press. Stitch down the side and across both ends. Attach a safety pin to one end and insert it through the opening in the side seam. Push it through the casing from the outside, back to the opening. Remove the safety pin, use the tie to draw up the bag, and then knot the ends for hanging.

TIE-UP SHADE

This pretty shade will brighten up any window. With its colorful underwater design, the fabric is ideal for children's bathrooms and was the source of inspiration for the fish decoration used elsewhere in our Deep Blue Sea Bathroom.

Backed with a coordinating polkadotted material, which is also used for the two pairs of ties that hold the shade up, it provides a cheerful way of blocking either the view or direct sunlight. It is also very easy to make.

The shade is simply attached to the top of the window frame (or to a mounting baord on the wall above) with a strip of Velcro®. This type of shade is most suited to windows where it won't need to be constantly raised and lowered, and where you do not need to block out the light totally. It is the perfect solution for bathroom windows that are not directly overlooked.

YOU WILL NEED

MAIN FABRIC FOR FRONT
COORDINATING FABRIC FOR BACK
MATCHING SEWING THREAD
SEW-AND-STICK VELCRO®

MEASURING

Measure the area you want the shade to cover and add 1in (2.5cm) to the width and 1½in (4cm) to the length for seams. The two pairs of ties will need to be this length plus extra for tying into bows.

1 Cut out a rectangle to the correct dimensions from the main fabric, and another from the backing fabric. Cut out four fabric strips for the ties, each to the desired length by a width of 4½in (11.5cm).

2 Fold each long fabric strip in half lengthwise, right sides together and raw edges even, and stitch a ¼in (6mm) seam down the long edge and across one end. Trim off the corners, turn right side out, and press.

3 Lay the backing piece right side up on a flat surface. Place two ties on top, one tie over the other, parallel to the long edge of the backing piece and with the unstitched ends even with the raw edge of the fabric. They should be one-quarter of the way in from the edge. Repeat for the other pair of ties,

placing them the same distance in from the opposite edge.

4 Place the main fabric piece on top, right side down, sandwiching the ties in between. Stitch a ½in (1.25cm) seam around the side and bottom edges, and a 1in (2.5cm) seam at the top edge, leaving an opening in the center of the top edge. The opening should be about one-third of the total width so it misses the ties.

5 Turn right side out, and press. Turn in the raw edges of the opening, and slipstitch to close. Allow one tie from each piece to hang down the front and the other down the back; baste in place at the top. Stitch the sew-on piece of a strip of Velcro® to the top edge. Remove the basting.

6 Stick the self-adhesive side of the Velcro® strip along the top of the window or batten. Roll up the shade by hand to the desired height and tie two nice big bows to hold it.

BATH MAT

Simple fish shapes are perfect to appliqué onto a plain bath mat. Just cut the shapes out of colored terrycloth, turn under a narrow hem around all edges, and slipstitch in place on the mat. Instead of terrycloth, you could use face cloths that match your bath towels.

Safe and Sound

The need to keep your children safe and protected in the home should always be balanced against their need to explore experiences and test their own capabilities.

However, there are many devices and much sensible advice available today which have helped reduce greatly the number of accidents occurring in the home.

KITCHEN

The kitchen is a potentially hazardous room, especially when toddlers are underfoot during food preparation or chores. A few sensible precautions can prevent serious mishaps.

Where possible, try to keep children and their toys away from the main areas of food preparation and cooking.

Flooring should be kept clean, dry, and free of toys. Do not have any loose rugs in the kitchen, where people move about constantly.

If choosing a new stove, consider buying an eye-level broiler, or a floor-standing stove with a well-insulated oven door and childproof knobs. Fit a guard around the stovetop and always turn in saucepan handles when cooking. Use the back burners rather than the front ones.

Always store bleach and other household detergents in a lockable cabinet or high up out of reach. Keep knives and other sharp tools, such as electric mixer blades, out of reach.

Do not store glasses or precious china at a low level. Either fit all your kitchen cabinets with child-resistant catches or store dangerous items up high and make it clear to children that they are not allowed to open certain cabinets.

Allocate one or two cabinets that are safe for them to open and explore. That way you will probably find they no longer try to discover the contents of the others – unless you leave the doors open. Store safe but interesting items there, such as light saucepans, wooden spoons, foil pie plates, and empty yogurt containers, changing the contents slightly now and then so they get a surprise when they return to it. Small cans of food or light plastic food containers would not harm children if they mistakenly opened a low cabinet.

In case of fire, a smoke detector should be installed nearby (but not actually in the kitchen), and a fire blanket and fire extinguisher should be kept in a safe place in the kitchen.

When small appliances are not in use, unplug them. Replace long cords with shorter, curly ones to make them less accessible to a child.

LIVING ROOMS

Most accidents in living rooms occur because of poorly guarded fireplaces or unsupervised children falling from furniture.

Avoid placing furniture near a fire, particularly if filled with polyurethane foam. This foam is no longer sold, because of the speed with which it catches fire and the toxic fumes it releases in the process, but it still exists in older furniture. Fireplaces that are used should always be protected with a screen that extends to each side of the hearth and can be screwed to the wall to prevent a child removing it.

Coffee tables should have rounded edges and no glass tops. When children are toddlers you may find it easier to move the coffee table out of sight for a while, as they will delight in trying to climb on, over, and under it at any opportunity. Use table corner protectors for any sharp, low-level shelves or units.

On wooden floors, make sure that rugs are fitted with a nonslip mat and that any varnish or floor polish does not make the floor unduly slippery. If your children are asthmatic or prone to eczema, wooden floors are better as they retain far less dust than wall-to-wall carpets.

Conceal the cords of freestanding lamps behind pieces of furniture where possible, and fit any unused electrical outlets with safety guards. Use cable clips to avoid dangling cords behind televisions and video recorders.

Keep all breakables and alcohol out of reach, on shelves or in cupboards. Bookcases that could be pulled over should be screwed to the wall. Consider fixing alcove shelves higher up the wall for storing precious items.

Glazed or French doors should be fitted with safety glass, or the existing glass covered with safety film. Put stickers on large areas of glass such as sliding glass doors to help prevent them from becoming "invisible." Casement windows should be fitted with locks to prevent small children from opening them and possibly even climbing through them. (Be sure to keep the keys nearby and clearly visible in case of fire.)

CHILDREN'S ROOMS

In the nursery, temperature control is very important, particularly during the winter months. Very tiny babies, under three months old, are unable to regulate their own body temperatures, so it is vital that the room is kept at a constant temperature during the first few weeks, ideally around 65–73 degrees Fahrenheit (19–22 degrees Celsius).

Do not place a crib too near a door or window where your baby could be exposed to drafts.

Make sure the crib conforms to safety regulations. The height from the top of the mattress to the top of the crib, the distance between the bars, the catch on the "drop side," the space between the mattress and the crib, the paint (if any), and the mattress itself are all covered by safety regulations. The bumper, if you have one tied around the sides of the crib, should have short ties so there is no danger of one becoming entwined around your baby's neck or of your baby swallowing one. Never give a baby that is less than one year old a pillow.

A baby alarm will give you peace of mind if the layout of your house tends to muffle the sound of a baby's crying.

Fit a dimmer switch to the overhead light in the nursery so you can check on your baby without disturbing him or her when you go to bed.

Diaper changing should be carried out on a flat, stable surface. A changing pad on the floor is the safest place, but this can give you backache, so you might decide to use a changing table or chest of drawers placed against a wall. A table or chest should ideally have a rim around the edge to help prevent the baby from falling. Never leave your baby unattended on any of these surfaces. Always finish changing a diaper before answering the doorbell, the telephone, or a demanding toddler.

As your child grows and needs a bed, you have various options open to you. Raised beds and bunk beds are great for children over five years old. A single bed can be protected with a guard on the side to insure that a two- or three-year-old does not fall out at night.

Use only small chests of drawers or bookcases screwed to the wall so they can't be pulled over.

Keep nappies, diaper cream, diaper buckets, and antiseptic cleaners out of reach of toddlers, in a lockable cabinet.

BATHROOMS

When children are around, try to keep all potentially dangerous bathroom chemicals, medicines, tablets, razor blades and razors, cosmetics, and so on in one place, ideally in a wall-mounted, lockable cabinet that is out of reach of the toilet and bathtub areas. Children can otherwise climb onto the toilet to gain access if it is left unlocked at any time.

Place a nonslip mat in the bath so babies and toddlers do not slide around too much at bathtime. If a shower has a glass screen or door, make sure it is made of safety glass.

HALLS AND STAIRS

Hallways and stairways should have adequate lighting so that everyone can climb the stairs safely at night. If you don't like to leave the hall light on all night, at least fit a plug-in night light. Use safety gates at the bottom and top of the stairs until your child can safely crawl up and can come down backward.

Check that your front door has an additional catch high up – either a chain or a bolt – so that children cannot suddenly run out onto the road.

GENERAL SAFETY

Fit a smoke detector in the nursery and check the batteries regularly.

When painting and decorating a child's room, bear in mind that the solvents in oil-based paints like eggshell and gloss emit pungent vapors during application. Always do any decorating of the nursery well in advance of a baby's arrival and with all windows open, since the fumes take some time to dissipate. Wherever possible, consider using water-based paints such as latex instead; they are safer.

Never leave power tools or other decorating implements around, either during or after a decorating task. Stencil paints, scrapers, and even sandpaper are all potentially hazardous in the wrong hands.

Make sure that the long strings on window shades and curtain pullers are knotted up well out of an inquisitive toddler's reach until he or she is old enough to know not to swing on them, play with them, or in any other way get tangled up in them.

TEMPLATES (OVERLEAF)

Enlarge the templates on pages 132–139 either by transferring square by square onto graph paper with squares of the size specified for each template, or by using a photocopier. The templates that are one-third actual size need to be enlarged to 300 percent, those that are one-half actual size to 200 percent, and those that are two-thirds actual size to 150 percent.

TEMPLATES

Owl and the Pussycat Bedroom: Moon and five-pointed star templates for stenciling tops of walls (page 48) and four-pointed star for design on Four-Poster Bed Frame (page 53). These templates are one-third actual size. I square = 4in (10cm).

Ducks Nursery: Large duck templates for Ducks and Flowers Wall Hanging (pages 42-3) and small duck template for stenciling inside cupboard (page 32). These templates are one-third actual size. I square = 4in (10cm).

Amazon Bedroom: Parakeet templates for Tie-Top Jungle Curtains (page 64). These templates are two-thirds actual size. I square = 2in (5cm).

Amazon Bedroom:
Crocodile template for
Appliquéd Swamp Rug (pages
66–7). This template is
one-third actual size.
1 square = 4in (10cm).
Align A–A on body with A–A
on head, and align B–B on body
with B–B on tail to make one
long template.

A ⸺ A

A ⸺ A

B ⸺ B

B ⸺ B

Amazon Bedroom: Waterlily templates
for Appliquéd Swamp Rug (pages 66–7).
These templates are one-third actual size.
1 square = 4in (10cm).

Sailor's Bedroom: Nautical templates for Customized Flags (page 76). These templates are two-thirds actual size.
I square = 2in (5cm).

Little Princess's Bedroom: Large scroll template for Stenciled Wallpaper Border (page 84) and small scroll template for Painted Decoration (door, page 86). These templates are one-half actual size. 1 square = 2in (5cm)

Creative Play Room: Numerals and alphabet templates for Color-by-Number Walls (page 110) and Hopscotch Floorcloth (page 106).

These templates are one-third actual size. 1 square = 4in (10cm).

Deep Blue Sea Bathroom:
Underwater life templates for Bath
Backsplash, Tropical Fish Cabinet,
Painted Decoration, and Height Chart
(pages 122–4). These templates are
two-thirds actual size.
1 square = 2in (5cm).

LAURA ASHLEY SHOPS

UNITED KINGDOM
LONDON SHOPS
Brent Cross 0181 202 2679
Covent Garden 0171 240 1997
Ealing 0181 579 5197
Kensington 0171 938 3751
Knightsbridge (clothes only)
 0171 823 9700
Knightsbridge (home
 furnishings only)
 0171 235 9797
Marble Arch 0171 355 1363
Oxford Circus 0171 437 9760

COUNTRY SHOPS
Aberdeen 01224 625787
Aylesbury 01296 84574
Banbury 01295 271295
Barnet 0181 449 9866
Bath 01225 460341
Bedford 01234 211416
Belfast 01232 233313
Beverley 01482 872444
Birmingham 0121 631 2842
Bishops Stortford
 01279 655613
Bournemouth (clothes only)
 01202 293764
Brighton 01273 205304
Bristol, Broadmead
 0117 922 1011
Bristol, Clifton 0117 927 7468
Bromley 0181 290 6620
Bury St Edmunds
 01284 755658
Cambridge 01223 351378
Canterbury 01227 450961
Cardiff 01222 340808
Carlisle 01228 48810
Chelmsford 01245 359602
Cheltenham 01242 580770
Chester (clothes only)
 01244 313964
Chester (home furnishings only)
 01244 316403
Chichester 01243 775255
Colchester 01206 562692
Derby 01332 361642
Dudley 01384 79730
Eastbourne 01323 411955
Edinburgh (clothes only)
 0131 225 1218
Edinburgh (home furnishings
 only) 0131 225 1121
Epsom 01372 739595

Exeter 01392 53949
Farnham 01252 712812
Gateshead 0191 493 2411
Glasgow 0141 226 5040
Guildford 01483 34152
Harrogate 01423 526799
Hereford 01432 272446
High Wycombe 01494 442394
Hitchin 01462 420445
Horsham 01403 259052
Ipswich 01473 216828
Isle of Man 01624 801213
Jersey 01534 608084
Kings Lynn 01553 768881
Kingston 0181 549 0055
Leamington Spa 01926 314584
Leeds 0113 245 0622
Leicester 01162 513165
Lincoln 01522 511611
Llanidloes 01686 412557
Maidstone 01622 750138
Manchester 0161 834 7335
Middlesbrough 01642 226034
Milton Keynes 01908 660190
Newcastle-Under-Lyme
 01782 662014
Newport I.O.W. 01983 821806
Northampton (clothes only)
 01604 231975
Norwich 01603 632958
Nottingham 01159 503366
Oxford 01865 791689
Perth 01738 623141
Peterborough 01733 311766
Plymouth 01752 268344
Preston 01772 202425
Reading 01734 594313
Richmond 0181 940 9556
Salisbury 01722 338383
Sheffield 0114 270 1855
Sheffield Meadowhall
 0114 256 8221
Shrewsbury 01743 351467
Skipton 01756 700301
Solihull 0121 704 4344
Southampton 01703 228944
Southport 01704 546214
St Albans 01727 864611
Stockport 0161 474 7927
Stratford-Upon-Avon
 01789 298852
Sutton 0181 643 9790
Sutton Coldfield
 0121 355 3671
Swindon 01793 641727

Taunton 01823 288202
Tenterden 01580 765188
Torquay 01803 291443
Truro 01872 223019
Tunbridge Wells
 01892 534431
Watford 01923 254411
Wilmslow 01625 535331
Winchester 01962 855716
Windsor (clothes only)
 01753 854345
Windsor (home furnishings
 only) 01753 831456
Worcester 01905 20177
Worthing 01903 205160
Yeovil 01935 79863
York 01904 627707

HOMEBASES
Within Sainsbury's Homebase
 House and Garden Centres
Basildon 01268 584088
Basingstoke 01256 469510
Bath 01225 339293
Blackheath 0181 856 9767
Bradford 01274 611929
Branksome 01202 768311
Brentford 0181 847 2214
Camberley 01276 686227
Cardiff 01222 499675
Catford 0181 461 0606
Chichester 01243 533373
Colchester 01206 869187
Coventry 01203 715901
Crawley 01293 538351
Crayford 01322 558614
Croydon 0181 684 8250
Derby 01332 291260
Enfield 0181 366 2236
Falkirk 01324 631551
Gloucester 01452 526806
Guildford 01483 304115
Harlow 01279 413355
Hatfield 01707 275837
Hedge End 01489 789797
Hull 01482 572434
Ilford 0181 590 0212
Ipswich 01473 721124
Kensington 0171 603 2285
Kingston 0181 949 7861
Leeds 0113 268 5010
Leicester 0116 254 6075
Luton 0582 593445
Maidstone 01622 715400
Milton Keynes 01908 692727

New Southgate 0181 368 1698
Newcastle-Under-Lyme
 01782 711752
Northampton 01604 234143
Norwich 01603 417474
Nottingham 0115 941 3885
Oldbury 0121 544 7333
Orpington 01689 890353
Oxford 01865 747979
Penge 0181 778 4214
Rayleigh Weir 01268 745374
Reading 01734 584572
Richmond 0181 876 2235
Rochester 01634 200088
Romford 01708 730326
Ruislip 0181 841 8858
Sheffield 0174 255 5175
Stockport 0161 474 7489
Swansea 01792 650935
Swindon 01793 487125
Tunbridge Wells
 01892 546646
Wakefield 01924 387011
Waltham Cross 01992 625275
Walthamstow 0181 531 8233
Watford 01923 252075
Wimbledon 0181 946 9802
Worcester 01905 420401
Worle 01934 512628
York 01904 643911

REPUBLIC OF IRELAND
Cork 00 3532 127 4070
Dublin 00 3531 679 5433

**UNITED STATES OF
 AMERICA**
Albany 518 452 4998
Ann Arbor 313 747 6620
Ardmore 610 896 0208
Arlington 703 415 2111
Atlanta-Lenox 404 231 0685
Atlanta-Perimeter
 770 395 6027
Austin 512 451 4036
Bal Harbor 305 864 5628
Beachwood 216 831 7621
Birch Run 517 624 9297
Birmingham 205 985 0090
Bluffton 803 837 2366
Boca Raton 407 368 5622
Boston 617 536 0505
Bridgewater 908 725 3700
Buffalo 716 681 8600
Burlington MA 617 272 4540

Burlington VT 802 658 5006
Carmel-by-the-Sea
  408 624 8095
Central Valley 914 928 4561
Charleston 803 723 3967
Charlotte 704 362 0926
Charlottesville 804 971 7707
Chattanooga 615 855 5496
Chestnut Hill 617 965 7640
Chicago 312 951 8004
Cincinnati 513 793 5535
Columbus 614 224 5057
Corte Madera 415 924 5770
Costa Mesa 714 545 9322
Cranston 401 946 1211
Dallas-Galleria 214 980 9858
Danbury 203 790 5068
Dayton 513 299 9007
Denver-Cherry Creek
  303 322 9401
Des Moines 515 243 8881
Destin 904 654 2626
Edina 612 920 2811
Fairfax 703 352 7960
Farmington 203 521 8967
Fort Lauderdale 305 563 2300
Fort Worth 817 346 4666
Freeport 207 865 3300
Germantown 901 756 7036
Gilroy 408 848 5470
Glendale 818 242 0428
Grand Rapids 616 942 6828
Greenville 302 575 1653
Greenwich 203 661 5678
Grosse Pointe 313 886 6960
Hackensack 201 488 0130
Hingham 617 740 4122
Honolulu 808 942 5200
Houston 713 871 9669
Houston/West Oaks
  713 558 6113
Indianapolis 317 848 9855
Jacksonville 904 358 7548
Jeffersonville 614 948 2016
Kansas City 816 931 0731
King of Prussia 610 354 9137
Knoxville 615 558 6385
Lake Forest 708 615 1405
Lancaster 717 397 7116
Lexington 606 253 1724
Little Rock 501 666 0272
Los Angeles 310 553 0807
Louisville 502 585 2424
Manhasset 516 365 4834
McLean 703 827 0074
Miami 305 233 8911
Milwaukee 114 347 1930
Minnetonka 612 546 4613

Montgomery 205 284 7011
Myrtle Beach 803 236 4244
Nashville 615 383 0131
New Haven 203 782 9436
New Orleans 504 522 9403
New York City/Westside
  212 496 5110
North Bethesda 301 984 3223
Northbrook 708 480 1660
Novi 313 348 9260
Oakbrook 708 572 9195
Oklahoma City 405 848 6252
Omaha 402 390 2085
Orlando 407 351 2785
Osage Beach 314 348 1333
Owings Mills 410 363 2455
Palm Beach 407 832 3188
Palm Beach Gardens
  407 624 5901
Palm Springs 619 322 2099
Palo Alto 415 328 0560
Phoenix 602 956 6043
Pittsburgh 412 367 8881
Pittsburgh 412 621 0735
Pleasanton 510 463 8714
Portland 503 224 0703
Prince William 703 474 3124
Princeton 609 683 4760
Raleigh 919 781 1076
Reading 215 373 5495
Redondo Beach 310 542 4436
Richmond 804 740 1406
Ridgeland 601 957 9063
Rochester 507 287 1073
Sacramento 916 923 5696
Salt Lake City 801 363 8408
San Antonio 512 377 2833
San Diego 619 234 0663
San Diego 619 452 6116
San Francisco 415 788 0190
San Marcos 512 396 5570
Santa Ana 714 834 1211
Santa Barbara 805 682 8878
Santa Clara 408 244 3551
Scarsdale 914 723 8500
Schaumberg 708 619 9110
Seattle 206 343 9637
Secausus 201 863 3066
Short Hills 201 467 5657
Skokie 708 673 6604
Southampton 516 287 2104
Stamford 203 324 1067
Stony Brook 516 689 6622
St Augustine 904 823 9533
St Louis 314 993 4410
Tampa 813 253 2177
Towson 410 825 0362
Troy 810 649 0890

Tulsa 918 749 5001
Walnut Creek 510 947 5920
Westport 203 226 7495
White Plains 914 686 3404
Williamsburg 804 229 0353
Winston Salem 919 760 3733
Winter Park 407 740 8900
Woodbury 516 367 2810
Woodland Hills 818 346 7560
Worthington 614 433 9011

MOTHER AND CHILD
  STORES
Birmingham 205 987 7566
Chestnut Hill 617 965 5687
Denver-Cherry Creek
  303 322 9403
Farmington-Hartford
  203 561 4870
Hackensack-Riverside
  201 342 1222
Houston 713 622 2262
Kansas City 816 931 2810
King of Prussia 610 354 9137
Princeton 609 683 1300
Redondo Beach 310 542 6228
Schaumberg 708 240 1910
Short Hills 201 564 9600
Stamford 203 359 9902
Tulsa 918 749 5001
Walnut Creek 510 947 3932

HOME FURNISHING
  STORES
Alexandria 701 739 2144
Ardmore 215 896 8293
Atlanta 404 842 0102
Boston 617 357 5151
Burlingame 415 344 1774
Costa Mesa 714 545 7927
Kansas City 816 531 8971
New York City 212 735 5000
Ridgewood 201 670 0868
Short Hills 201 912 9150
Washington 202 686 1200

CANADA
Willowdale 416 223 9507
Calgary, Alberta 403 269 4090
London, Ontario 519 434 1703
Montreal 514 284 9225
Ottawa 613 238 4882
Quebec 418 659 6660
Sherway Gardens, Etobicoke
  416 620 7222
Toronto 416 922 7761
Toronto-Yorkdale
  416 256 2040

Vancouver 604 688 8729
Winnipeg 204 943 3093

AUSTRIA
Graz 0316 844398
Innsbruck
  0152 579254/579257
Linz 070 797700
Salzburg 0662 840344
Vienna 01 5129312

BELGIUM
Antwerp 03 2343461
Bruges 050 349059
Brussels (clothes only)
  02 5112813
Brussels (home furnishings
  only) 02 5120447
Gent 092 240819

FRANCE
Paris
94 rue de Rennes
  1 45 48 43 89
95 Avenue Raymond Poincaré
  1 45 01 24 73
261 rue Saint Honoré
  1 42 86 84 13
Galeries Lafayette, 40 bld
  Haussmann
  second floor (clothes only)
  1 42 82 34 56
  fifth floor (home furnishings
  only) 1 42 82 04 11
Au Printemps, 64 bld
  Haussmann
  second floor (clothes only)
  1 42 82 52 10
  seventh floor (home
  furnishings only)
  1 42 82 44 20
Au Printemps, Centre
  Commercial Vélizy
  Avenue de L'Europe, Vélizy,
  Villacoublay
  Niveau 2 (clothes and home
  furnishings) 1 30 70 87 66
Au Printemps, Centre
  Commercial
  Parly 2
  Avenue Charles de Gaulle,
  Le Chesnay
  Niveau 1 (home furnishings
  only) 1 39 54 22 44
  ext. NR 247
  Niveau 2 (clothes only)
  1 39 54 22 44 ext. NR321
Aix-en-Provence 42 27 31 92

Bordeaux 56 44 10 30
Clermont-Ferrand 73 31 22 05
Dijon 80 30 04 44
Lille 20 06 90 06
Lyon 78 37 18 19
Montpellier 67 60 75 75
Nancy 83 35 21 09
Nantes 40 73 17 18
Nice 93 16 06 93
Rouen 35 70 20 02
Strasbourg 88 75 18 90
Toulon 94 21 89 58
Toulouse 61 21 38 85

GERMANY
Augsburg 0821 154021
Berlin (home furnishings only)
  030 8826201
Berlin (clothes only)
  030 8824934
Berlin (Kadewe) 030 2183016
Bielefeld 0521 177188
Bonn 0228 654908
Bremen 0421 170443
Cologne 0221 2580470
Dortmund 0231 141009
Düsseldorf 0211 327000
Essen 0201 200482
Frankfurt 069 288791
Hamburg 040 371173
Hanover 0511 326919
Heidelberg 06 22 1189851
Karlsruhe 0721 25968
Munich 089 2608224
Münster 0251 42272
Nürenberg 0911 2451819
Stuttgart 0711 2261064
Wiesbaden 0611 302086

ITALY
Milan 02 86463532

LUXEMBOURG
Luxembourg 221 320

NETHERLANDS
Amsterdam 020 6228087
Arnhem 026 4430250
Eindhoven 040 2435022
Groningen 050 3185060
The Hague 070 3600540
Maastricht 043 3250972
Rotterdam 010 4148535
Utrecht 030 2313051

SPAIN
Barcelona 93 4125490

SWITZERLAND
Basel 061 2619757
Bern 031 3120696
Geneva (clothes only)
  022 33113494
Geneva (home furnishings only)
  022 33103048
Zurich 01 2211394

ASIA
HONG KONG SHOPS IN
  SHOPS
Sogo 852 2891 1767

JAPAN
Ginza 03 3571 5011
Yagoto 052 836 7086
Kichijoji 0422 21 1203
Jiyugaoka 03 3724 0051
Jiyugaoka G (home furnishings
  only) 03 5701 5471
Yokohama LMP 045 222 5308
Futako Tamagawa
  03 3708 3151
Gifu Melsa 0582 66 3136

Fukuoka Tenjin 092 716 7415
Sapporo Factory 011 207 4031

SHOPS IN SHOPS
TOKYO
Mitsukoshi Nihonbashi
  03 3241 5617
Mitsukoshi Ikebukuro
  03 3987 6074
Tokyu 03 3477 3836
Keio Shinjuku 03 3344 0080
Mitsukoshi Ginza
  03 3561 4050
Tobu Ikebukuro 03 3980 0041

REST OF JAPAN
Mitsukoshi Yokohama
  045 323 1683
Saikaya Kawasaki
  044 211 8581
Saikaya Yokosuka
  046 823 1234
Chiba Mitsukoshi
  043 227 4731
Mitsukoshi Bandai
  025 243 6333
Sapporo Tokyu 011 212 2658
Kintetsu Abeno 06 625 2332
Hankyu Umeda 06 365 0793
Kawanishi Hankyu
  0727 56 1622
Mitsukoshi Hiroshima
  082 241 5055
Hiroshima Sogo 082 225 2955
Hakata Izutsuya 092 452 2181
Nagoya Mitsukoshi
  052 252 1838
Matsuzakaya Nagoyecki
  052 565 4339
Seishin Sogo 078 992 1586
Kobe Ilankyu 078 360 7528

Daimaru Kobe 078 333 4079
Tama Sogo 0423 39 2450
Kintetsu Kyoto 075 365 8024
Be Me Machida Daimaru
  0427 24 8174
Sanyo Himeji 0792 23 4792
Tenmaya Fukuyama
  0849 27 2214
Mitsukoshi Matsuyama
  0899 46 4829
Saikaya Fujisawa 0466 27 1111
Matsuzakaya Yokkaichi
  0593 551241
Cita Tokiwa 0975 33 1741
Bon Belta Narita 0476 23 3236
Hamamatsu Matsubishi
  053 452 2941
Kagoshima Mitsukoshi
  0992 39 4635
Saga Tamaya 0952 28 0608
Kintetsu Nara 0742 30 2751
Kokura Izutsuya 093 522 2627
Kyoto Takashimaya
  075 252 7952

SINGAPORE
SHOPS IN SHOPS
Sogo 65 334 1014
Isetan Scotts 65 735 0495

TAIWAN
SHOPS IN SHOPS
Ta-Lee Isetan 886 7 241 8860
Pacific Sogo 886 2 740 9662
Shin Kong Mitsukoshi
  886 2 382 4859

ACKNOWLEDGMENTS

The author would like to thank the RoSPA (Royal Society for the Prevention of Accidents) and Claire, Robert, and Christopher Cooper for their assistance.

The publishers would like to thank Mary Batten, Jemima Dyson, Chris Churchley, Denize Lohan, Linda Bramble, Kerry Skinner, and Martin Sherman for their help in the production of this book.

The publishers would also like to thank the following, who kindly loaned props for the photographs: The Conran Shop, London, tel 0171-589 7401 (bedspread, rug, embroidered cushions, canopy on pp 92-103); Far Away Trading, London, tel 0171-738 9420 (metal coat and hat hooks, candlesticks, coffee table on pp 92-103); The Holding Company, London, tel 0171-352 7495 (toy box on p 60, chest on p 115, and towel rail and cabinet on p 123); David Shields, London, tel 0181-858 3534 or 0171-731 7913 (3D ship picture in bleached wood frame on p 68).

The photographs on pages 3, 7, 8-9, 10, 13, 15, 16, 19, 35 and 37 are from the Laura Ashley Archives. All other photographs are by Lucinda Symons.

INDEX

Page numbers in *italics* refer to templates.